Index

10472263

Introduction

"It is well to have water in your neighborhood, to give buoyancy to and float the earth. One value even of the smallest well is, that when you look into it you see that earth is not continent but insular." – Henry David Thoreau, *Walden*

A piece of what Thoreau might have called "dry land" in the middle of New York Harbor, Governors Island is a powerful site especially for creative minds. And artists, like the water he describes, have also been known to make us look at things in new and different ways. It is for these reasons, at the beginning of a new era for an island with a densely layered history 800 yards from a profoundly complex city, that it is vitally important to have space there for artists to create and share new work.

Building 110: LMCC's Arts Center at Governors Island, with the harbor on one side and parkland on the other, houses a gallery, 20 visual arts studios, and two rehearsal spaces. An Army warehouse built in 1879, Lower Manhattan Cultural Council (LMCC) transformed historic Building 110 into a multi-use arts facility for the development and presentation of new work by visual and performing artists. Artists in LMCC's residency programs at Governors Island are uniquely positioned to explore, interpret, and imagine the past, present, and future of this unparalleled site. Likewise, through open studio events, audiences gain access to a creative process that typically happens behind closed doors.

The 20 artists represented in this catalogue worked together in Building 110 from August to December 2012. Their practices are diverse and yet each project is inextricably specific to the site in some way. From Jenifer Wightman's bacteria paintings to Alan Ruiz's re-contextualization of LMCC's studio wall system to Abraham Storer's plein-air paintings to Jeanne Verdoux's found-object project *Mr. Bones*, each artist also calls on the viewer to rethink or reconsider something, be it an object, a perspective, or a scientific process.

When Sandy hit, this particular group of artists confronted a singular challenge. We were fortunate that the Island and Building 110 came through relatively unscathed, but post-Sandy restarting their residencies took time and we were without heat. Proving ever-resilient, the artists persevered through chilly December and remained committed to making their work.

These artists have had a transformative experience in five months of working at Governors Island but they too have had a transformative effect on the place, participating in its future by charting its present.

Melissa Levin
DIRECTOR OF CULTURAL PROGRAMS
Lower Manhattan Cultural Council

Ruta Butkute

Ruta Butkute approaches the island through the use of video. She refers to her use of the medium as "sculptural video". Her short experimental films function as visual thoughts and experiences of Governors Island. A sense of physicality and a continuous tension between architectural and natural forms are characteristic of these works. Butkute sees her videos as research into the visual relation between functional and free (non- functional) form. Through often simple transformations of looking and a sense of the poetic language of space, Butkute reminds the

viewer of the proximity of the natural world and the constant friction with the urban landscape. Translating form into form, her work calls to mind Ranciere's "poetic labour of translation". In his thoughts on learning he describes how one can learn an entire language by only knowing one poem; "By observing and comparing one thing with another, a sign with a fact, a sign with another sign. One learns everything in the same way as one initially learns its mother tongue, as one learns to venture into the forest of things and signs surrounding it."

Anaphora, 2012, video still

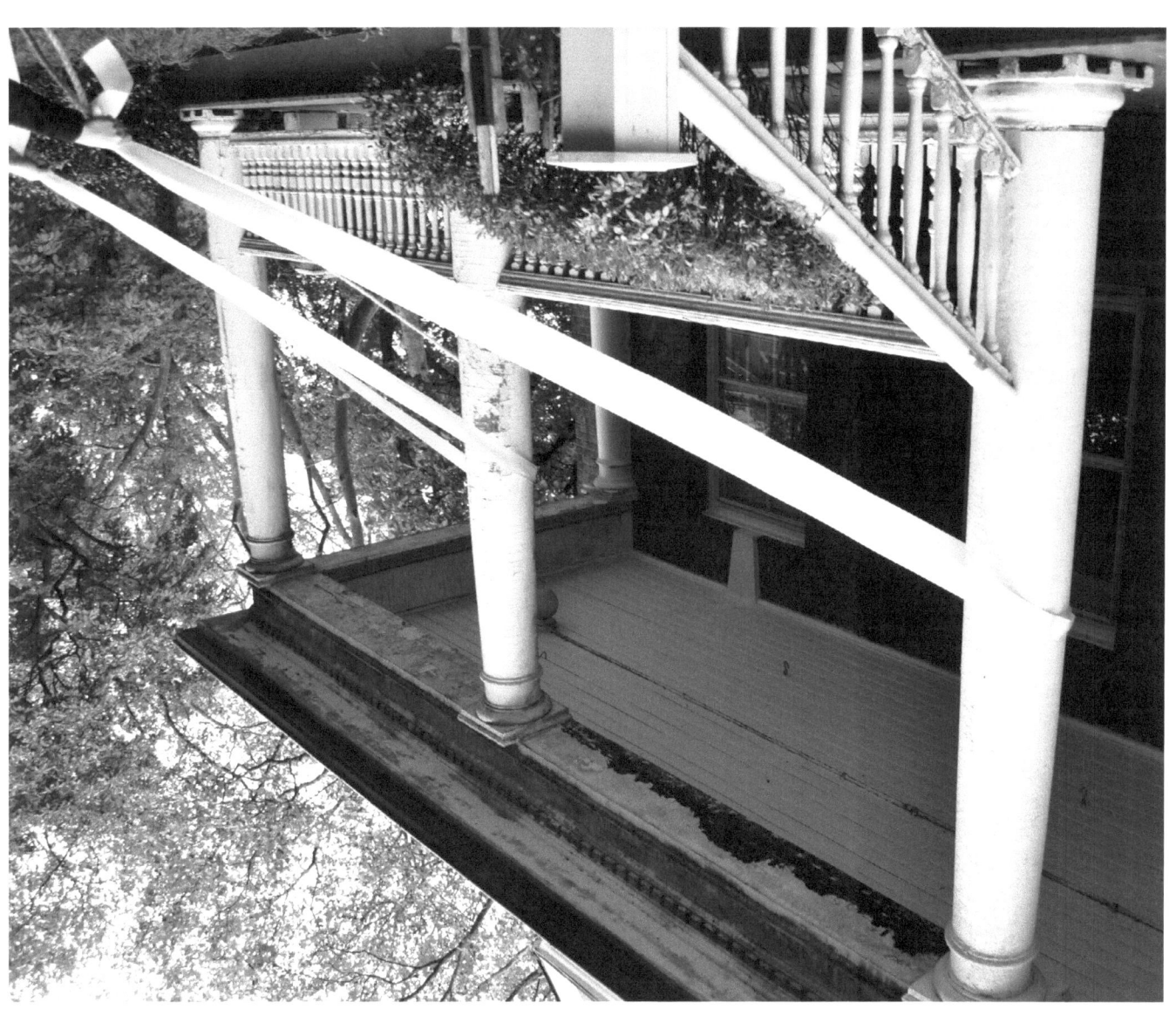

5

Jessica Cannon

While on Governors Island Jessica Cannon
created a series of new works on paper based
on encounters with the landscape: the old stone
walls, electric palm trees, ships, and the Island
itself.

Her experience of working on the Island evoked
feelings of isolation as well as immersion.
The works created during this time are derived
from that experience and incorporate aspects
of the Island into broader psychic landscapes.

Island Within An Island, Acrylic on paper, 30" x 40", 2012

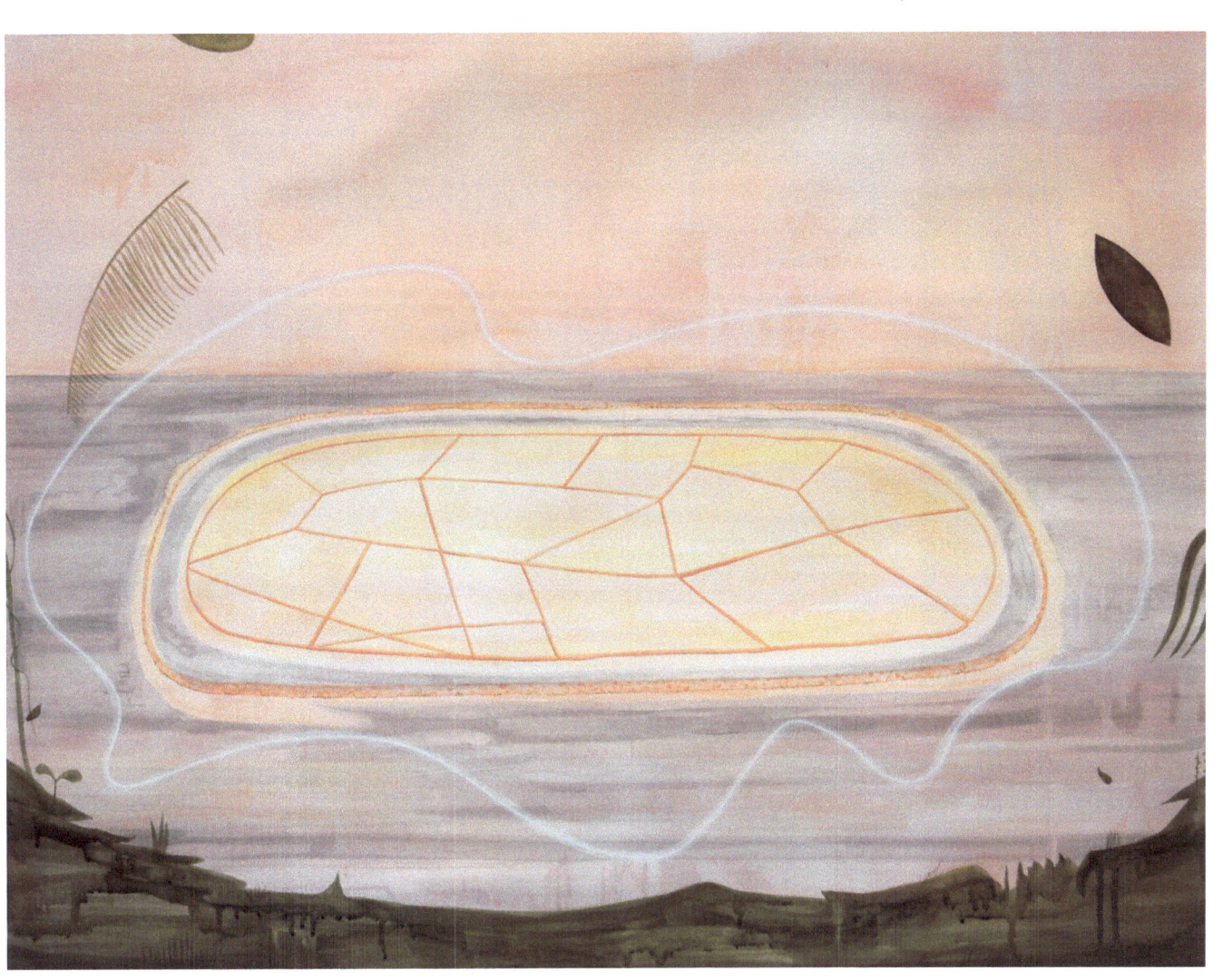

Maya Ciarrocchi

During her residency on Governors Island Ms. Ciarrocchi completed *Overburden*, a single channel video installation centered on Mountaintop Removal mining in West Virginia. The work is comprised of durational images of active and abandoned mines juxtaposed with video portraits of activists, local residents, and miners. These images reflect the conflicting realities of life in West Virginia: the lushness of the landscape and the desolation of the mines. Through extended video portraits viewers can reflect on the people and through landscape portraits viewers are given the natural, eternal environment around them.

In addition to completing *Overburden* during her residency, Ms. Ciarrocchi began work on a new video project centered on individuals who have been raised in ultra-Orthodox Jewish communities and have left or are in the process of leaving these environments in order to enter the secular world.

Production still from *Overburden*, 2012,
HD video, 20 minutes

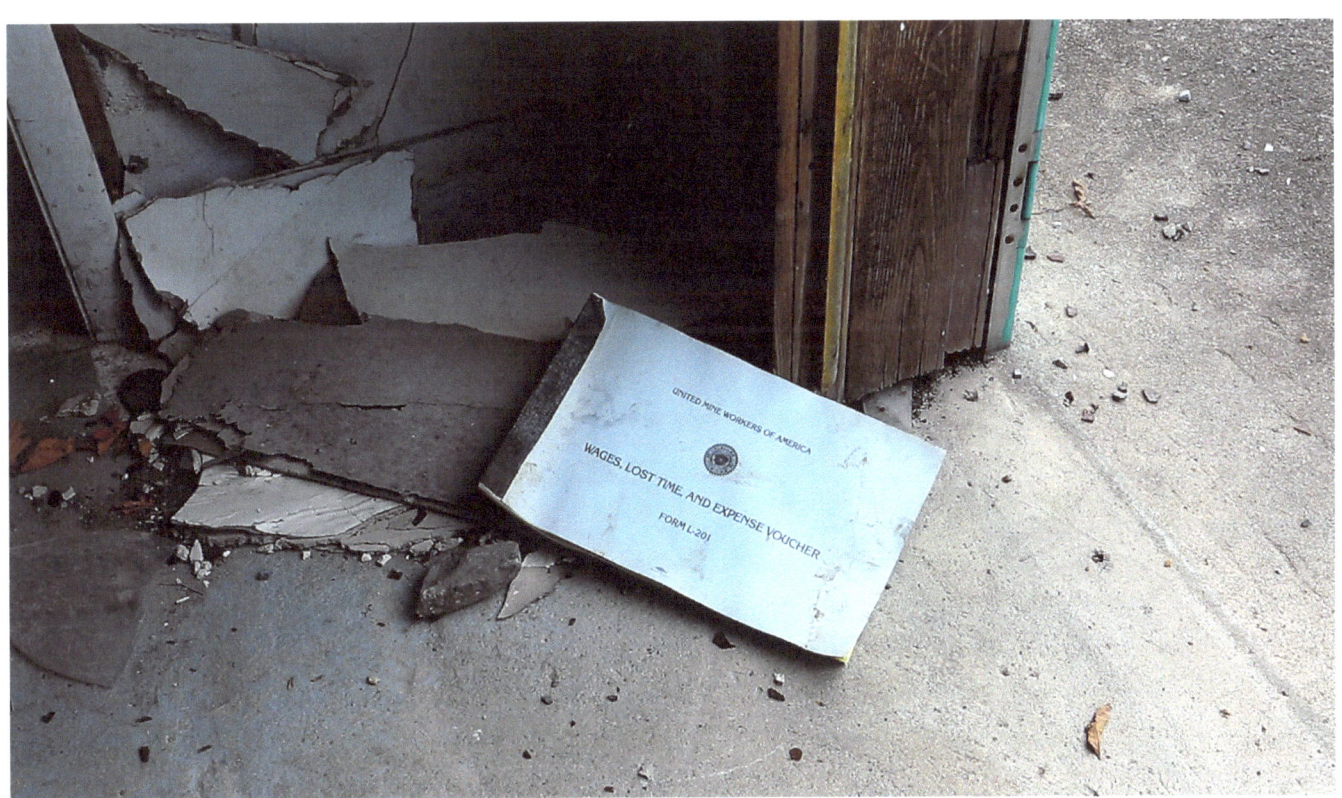

Abigail DeVille

In this time of night - buried beneath black and
white - soil, waste, rust and bodies experience
gray mist and gray silence. A great abandoned
hole that had been the site of Lincoln Heights.
The orientation is flipped and the alien finds
herself reaching downward from the night
toward the black ooze. Bodies sink and drown,
until running back to the dark, and the cold
and the present. All that was left, a drop of
infinite depth.

During her Swing Space residency at Governors
Island DeVille developed five off site-specific
installations in Red Hook Brooklyn, Los Angeles,
the Bronx, Kiev Ukraine, and Harlem, NY.
DeVille used her space at Governors Island as a
place of experimentation and a sounding board
for all of these multi layered installations.

"If I don't think I'm sinking, look what a hole I'm in", 2012
Medium: accumulated debris, free Craig's list materials,
plastic tarps, scavenged materials,
Dimensions: 385.6 sq. ft.

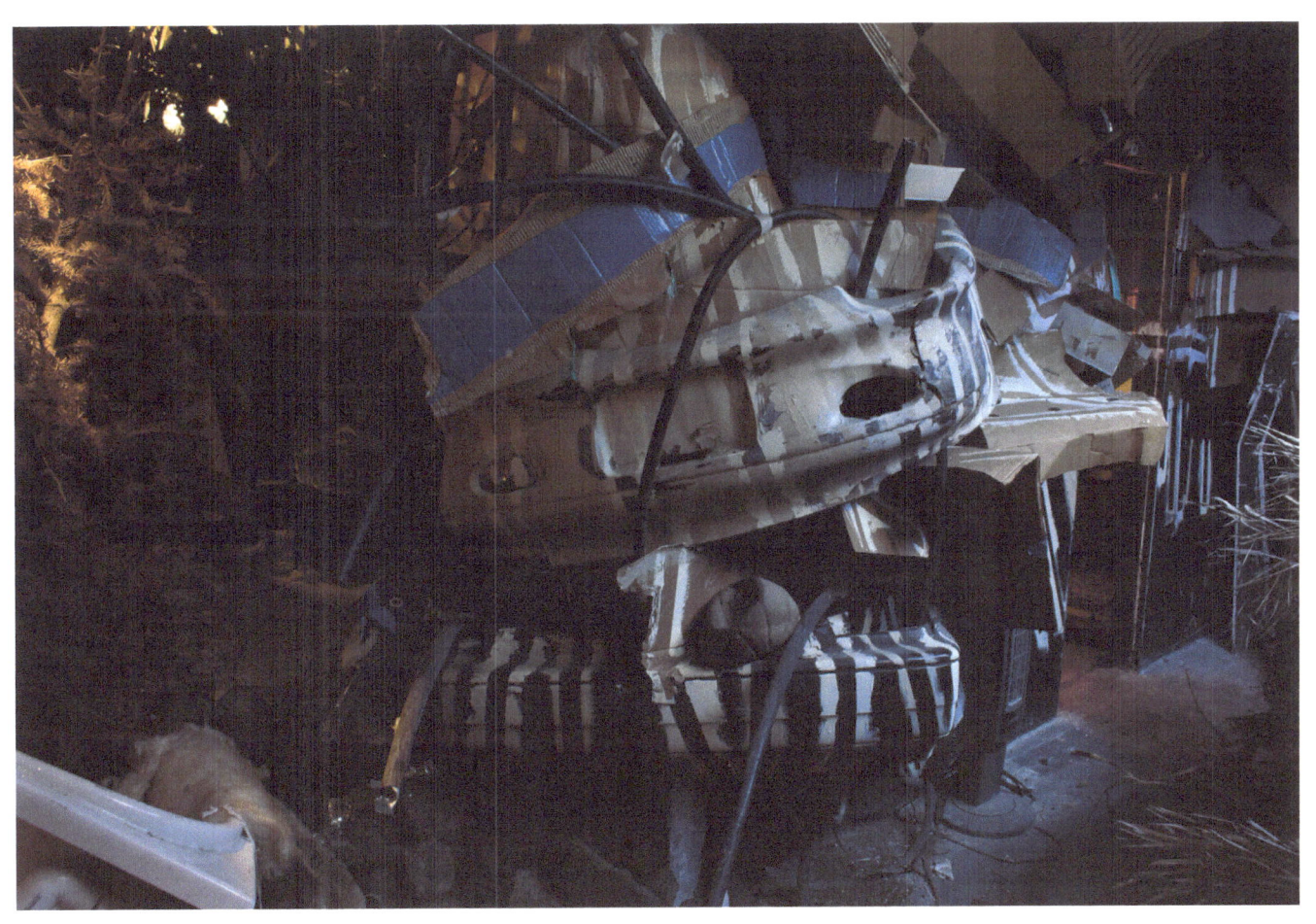

Elizabeth Duffy

Two of Governors Island's historic buildings inspired the installations Elizabeth Duffy created while in residence. The abandoned office spaces and tawdry function rooms of Pershing Hall, and the Admiral's House, a refined federal brick mansion, convey the sense of compressed time and contradictory experience that make the atmosphere of the island so particular and unsettling. The offices upstairs at Pershing Hall have a sense of post-apocalyptic abandonment. Pompous curtainsand the occasional dry-erase board are the only remaining embellishments; computer cables hang from walls impotent; soiled industrial carpets and lights left on suggest a remote human presence. An envelope Duffy found on the floor felt like treasure, and became the source for an installation. Across the esplanade on Nolan Park, the imposing Admiral's House is the material expression of domestic elegance and comfort that defined 19th century bourgeois culture: high ceilings, ornate woodwork, servants' quarters. A pair of gargantuan cannons guarding the entry suggest the boundary between protection and confinement is small.

Using sites on Governors Island as a point of departure in making new work allowed Duffy to explore the range of emotional states these eloquent spaces communicate, and to reacquaint herself with pivotal events in her own family history: the sense of dislocation that came out of growing up in a military family (Governors Island was formerly home to the Coast Guard, and its facilities still convey the hierarchical structure and impermanence that characterize that life), and the recognition that nearly 100 years ago Duffy's four grandparents traveled from Ireland through this harbor to New York. Facing lower Manhattan, center of the financial world and symbol of the sprawling wealth and class divisions that define our present culture, these vacant buildings draw attention to the restlessness, anxiety and sense of longing that are precursors to change.

Elizabeth Duffy creates installations using the patterning inside security envelopes, to evoke the comforting past of domestic house museums or the alienation of furniture showrooms. Using drawing, sculpture, installation, craft and digital media she creates an immersive experience that blurs the space between present, past and future; between reality, nostalgia and desire.

Detail of Envelop; verb [trans.] Warp/Weft Envelope Installation, 2012, dimensions variable, mixed media

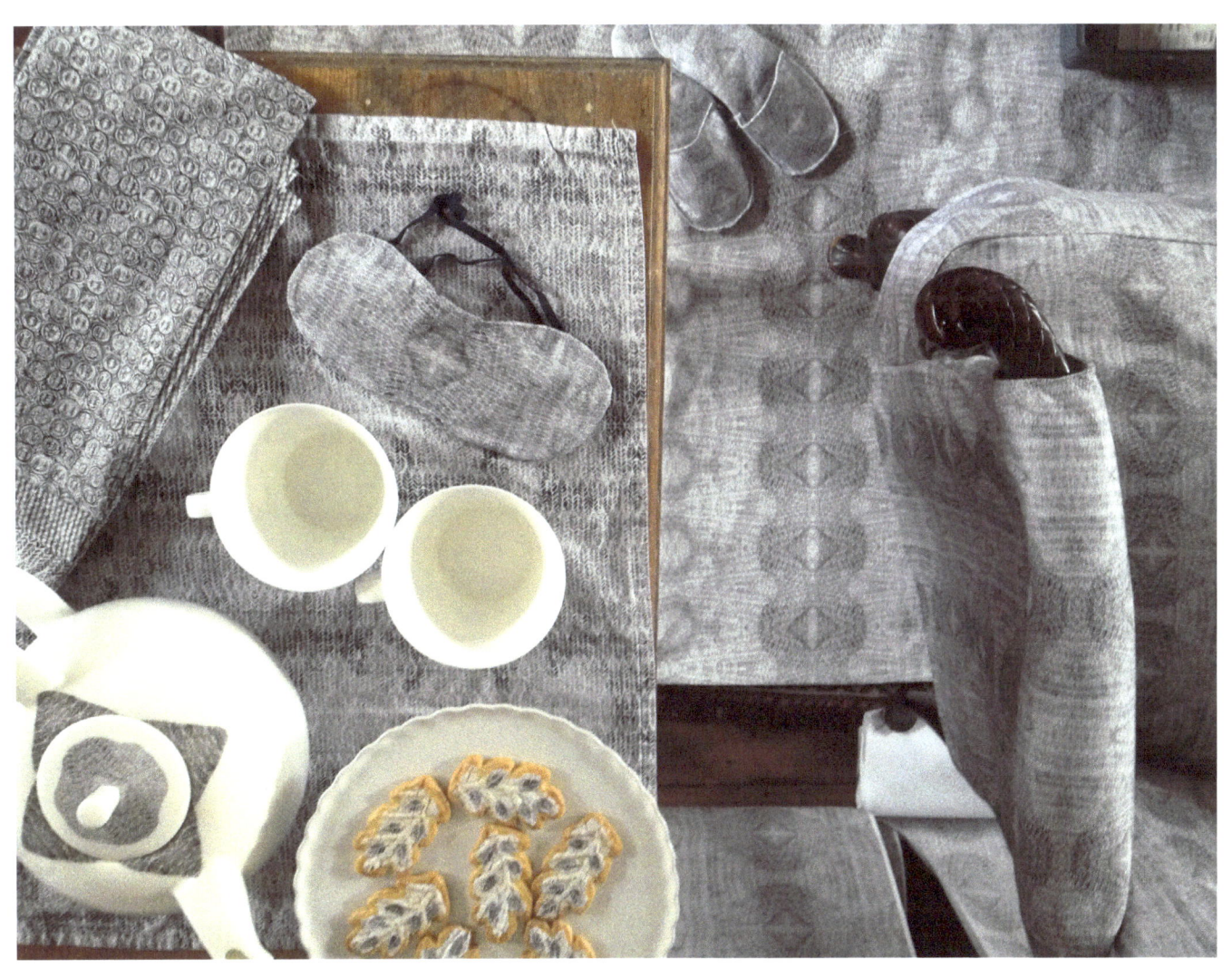

Erin Dunn

Using the island as a dancing ground Erin Dunn choreographed a series of dances inspired by the historic location and waterway. Her short 911 Dance is a reaction to the seasonally deserted island with uncannily private views of lower Manhattan. Moved by histories from colonial settlement to 911, Dunn danced to mourn and celebrate.

Untitled, 2012, Airbrush on felt, 48 x 40 in.

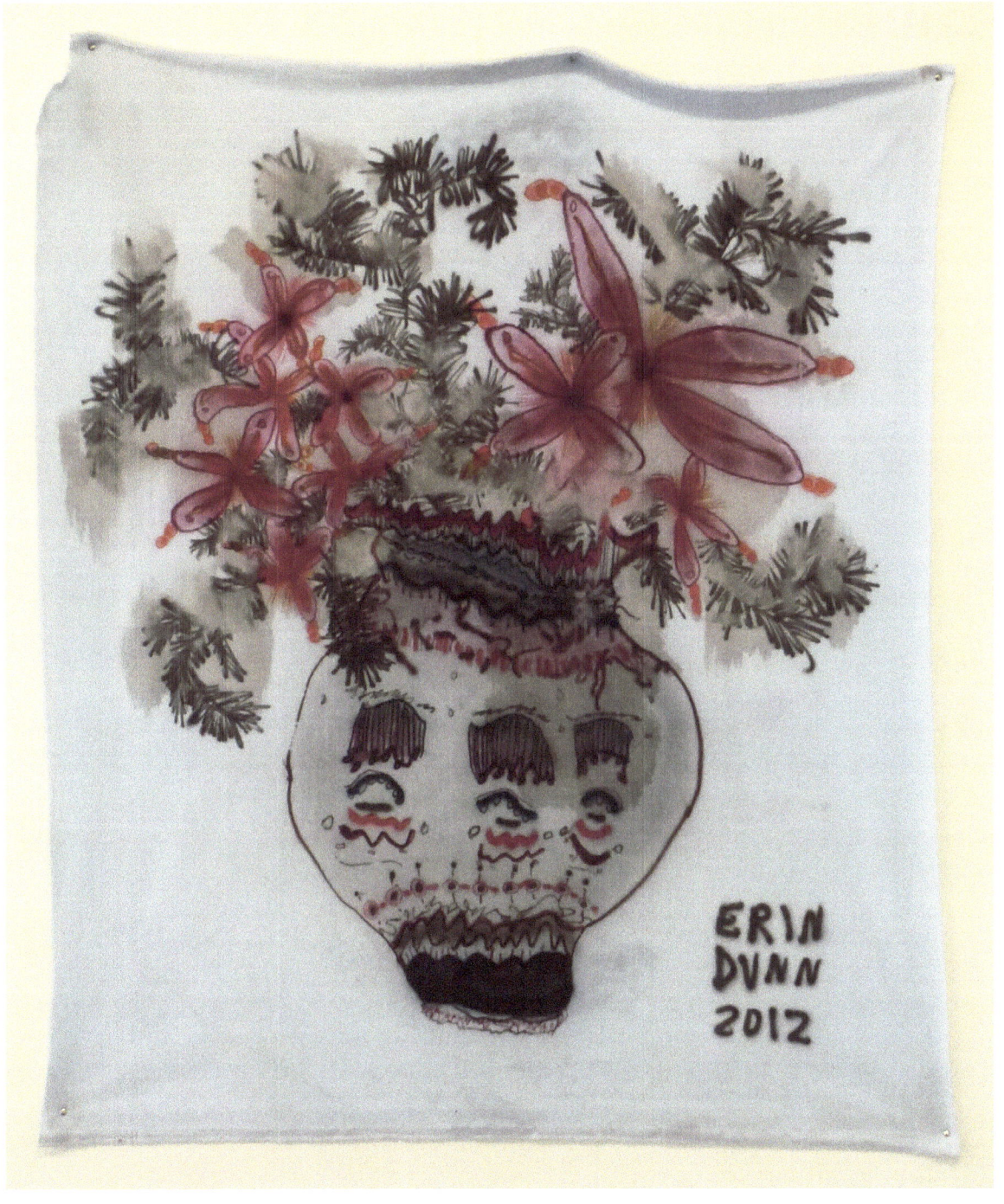

Laurie Frick

What if one could program a series of sensors, cameras, and GPS systems to log an individual's every move and then, assemble all of these movements into one cumulative display? One can imagine, depending on time, purpose, and energy, this scheme taking shape on a very substantial and large scale. In her exhibition Making Tracks, Laurie Frick does just this; conducting experiments with self-tracking and surveillance, and gathering a 90 day track using smartphone apps, accelerometers and sensors such as fitbit, openpaths and an iphone camera. During the LMCC residency, she collected her daily commute from Brooklyn over bridges to Lower Manhattan and across the harbor via ferry service to Governors Island. Frick presents her movements in one giant site-specific display, composed of a floor to ceiling grid of wood, littered with symbolic blocks of saturated color samples tracking the accumulation of her whereabouts.

Making Tracks (installation in the artist's studio as work in progress) | 2012 13 ft x 40 ft | Alumacore, cut wood panels and Abet Laminati samples

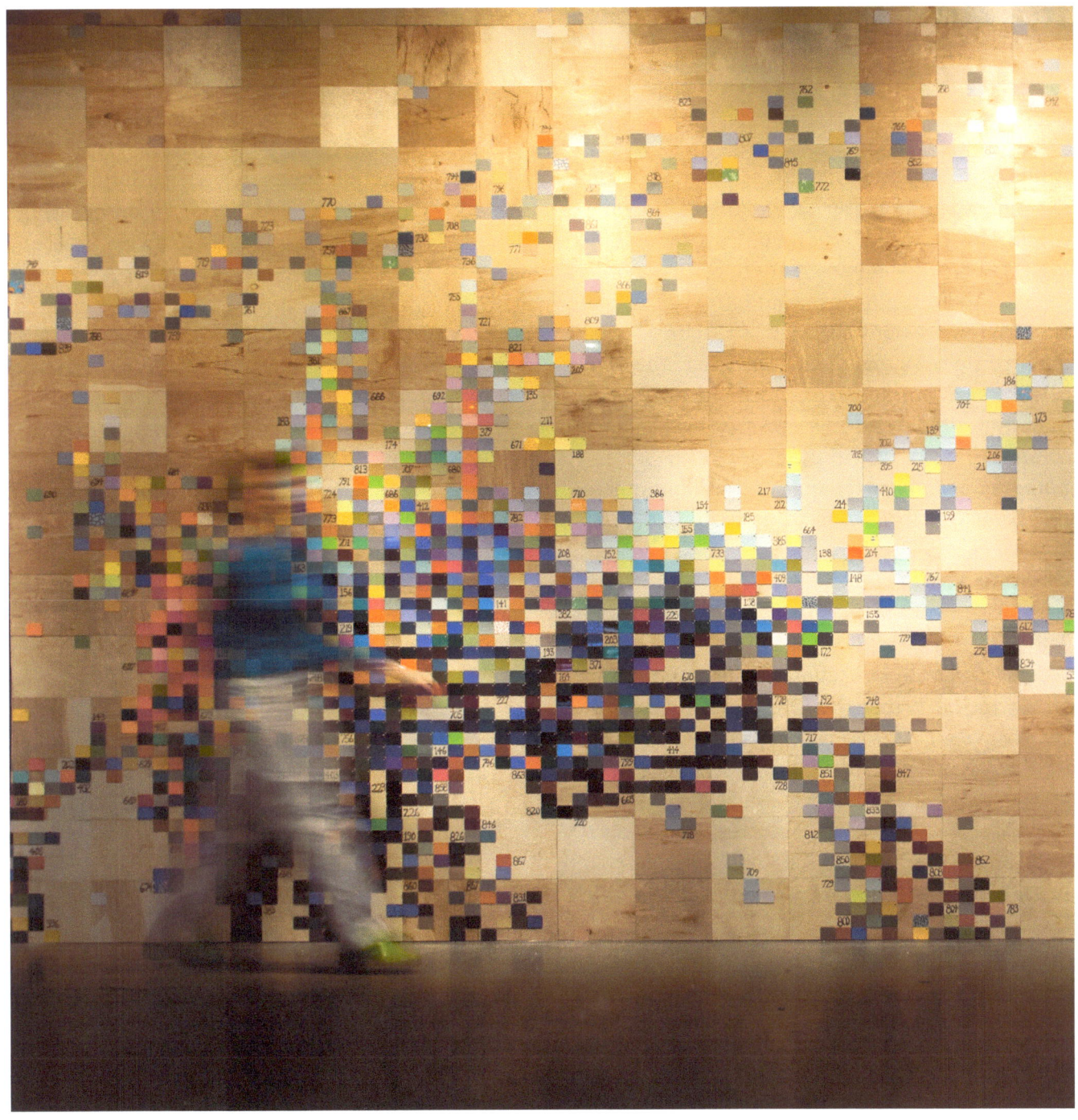

Marina Gutierrez

A persistent fascination with ocean, migration, environment and historical narrative drew me to the LMCC harbor studios of Governors Island, the ideal venue to create a 'Drawing Water' project. Following a somewhat quirky progression from a previous series of 'En Aqua Memoriam' sculptures and video, 'Drawing Water' is celebratory, interactive and alchemical. On this maritime site, an historic crossroads of conquest, commerce and cultural interaction, the performance of a simple exchange of word and image, recalls us to our place in living history.

Drawing Water

The plan: 1. **Build a boat**, a Boat-Mobile, a rolling studio/ work station/ performance prop with which to cruise the island. 2. **Compose a Survey** to gather visitors written memories and narratives of water, along with responses to a graph of images, symbols of maritime exchange specific to continents and cultures. 3. **Offer an exchange** .....would you like to fill out a survey in exchange for original signed artwork?.... and invite respondents to select a symbol rubbing, in the color of their choice. 4. **Precipitate Images** using surveys as biographical source material, via citing geography, illustrating narrative fragments and employing selections of exchange symbols. Fetch buckets of harbor salt water to fill trays. Immerse paper with copper and ferrous symbol silhouettes. Over time, the accumulating layers of blue/green oxidization and rust create images - Drawing Water.

Voyages of the Boat-Mobile – On September weekends I cruised Governors Island gathering narratives in over 200 surveys. Park visitors old, young, female, male, from the Americas, Asia, Europe, Africa and Australia contributed stories of migration, memories of, or relationships to water and affinities or aversions to a set of symbols. Each participant received, in exchange, a small work of art. See photos opposite page (bottom right – survey: text & symbols and bottom left – studio tests of precipitated drawing)

Drawing Water, 2012, project photos,172 acres

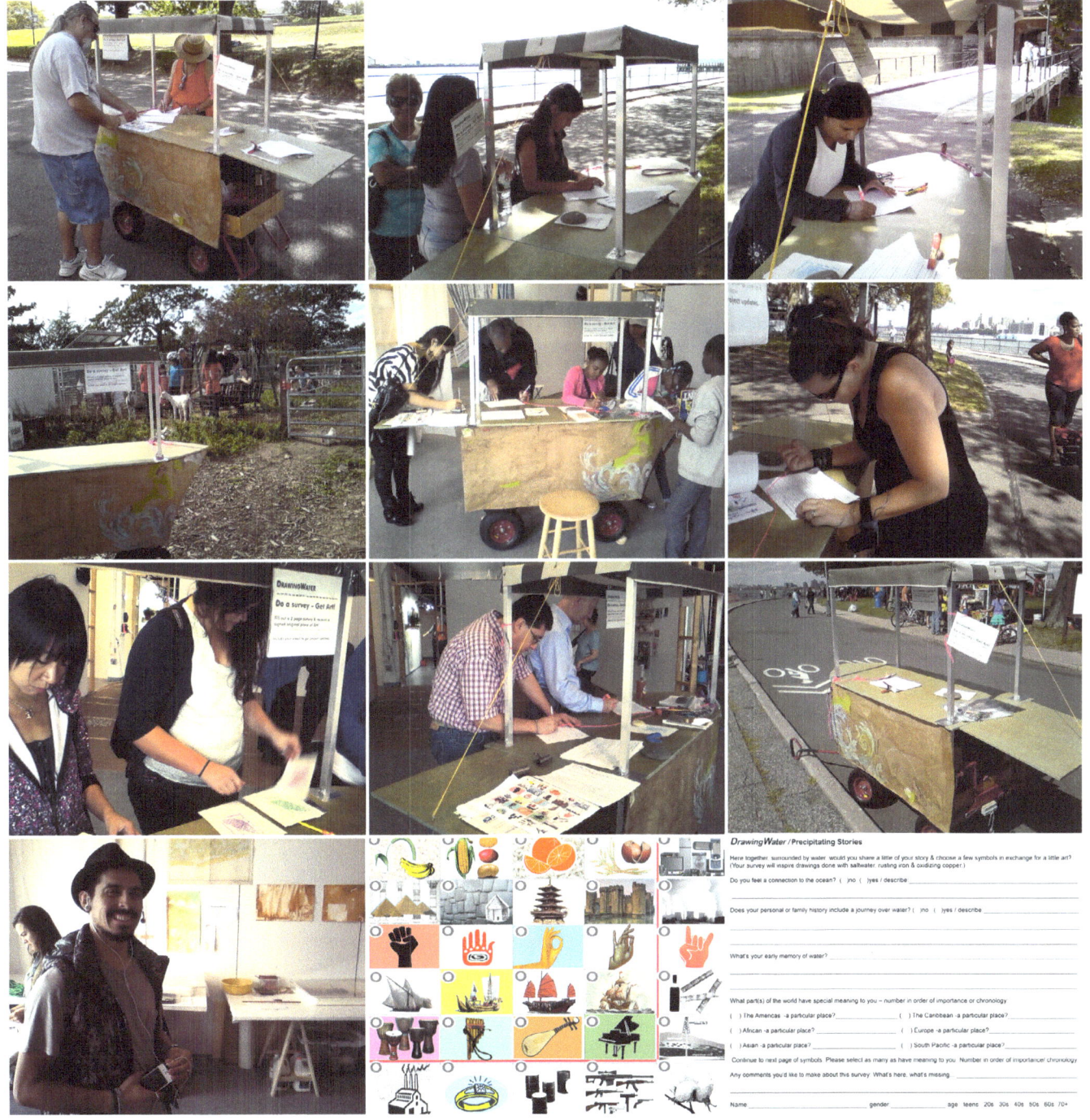

DrawingWater / Precipitating Stories

Here together, surrounded by water, would you share a little of your story & choose a few symbols in exchange for a little art? (Your survey will inspire drawings done with saltwater, rusting iron & oxidizing copper.)

Do you feel a connection to the ocean? ( )no ( )yes / describe _____

Does your personal or family history include a journey over water? ( )no ( )yes / describe _____
_____

What's your early memory of water? _____
_____

What part(s) of the world have special meaning to you – number in order of importance or chronology

( ) The Americas -a particular place?_____ ( ) The Caribbean -a particular place?_____

( ) African -a particular place?_____ ( ) Europe -a particular place?_____

( ) Asian -a particular place?_____ ( ) South Pacific -a particular place?_____

Continue to next page of symbols. Please select as many as have meaning to you. Number in order of importance/ chronology.

Any comments you'd like to make about this survey. What's here, what's missing. _____

Name _____ gender _____ age teens 20s 30s 40s 50s 60s 70+

Sarah Kabot

During her LMCC Swing Space residency, Sarah has been exploring the many markers of habitation, memorial and dedication present on Governors Island.

Two particular nodes of her inquiry have been the sites of St. Cornelius Chapel and the Coast Guard library. These sites stand out as relics of by- gone eras, by-gone populations. Within these structures idiosyncratic forms exist beside standardized systems of military and religious architecture. The complexities of individuated histories are inscribed in the objects that populate these places, in the form of commemoration. Names carved into stone and bronze plaques are abundant, and most often not available for regular public view.

As the former military base undergoes intense dismantling and reinvention, the significance of these emblems is shifting. Sarah's drawings, sculptures and installations examine the content of these locations within the fluctuating context of the island.

Pile Archival Inkjet Print, Glue 24" x 24" x 4", 2012

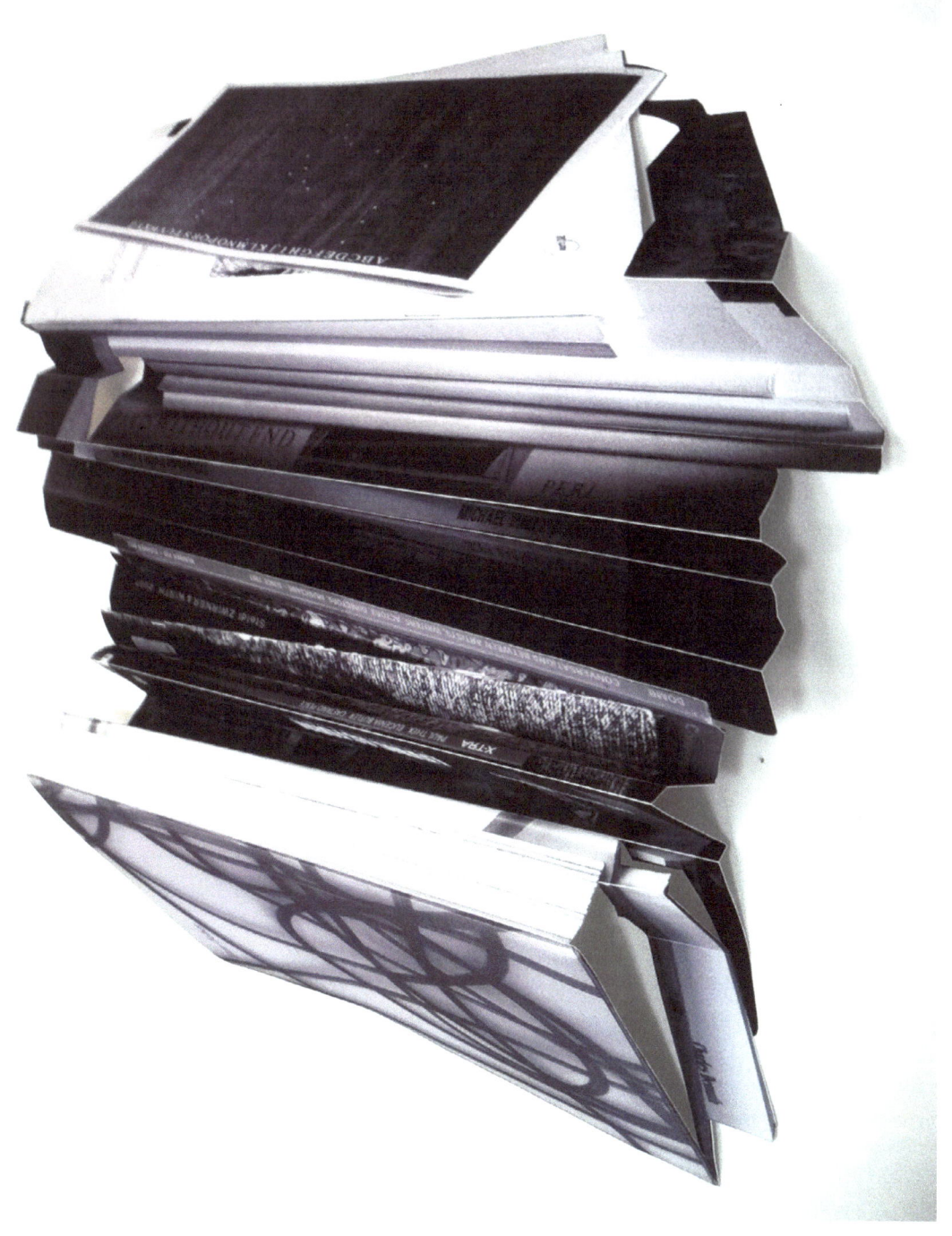

Jenn Kahn

Hang in there, Baby highlights the visual tension between the low art of kitsch and the high art symbolism of paint. Cherubs embody a curiously unfixed iconography. A pictorial symbol of passion, the figure exists simultaneously as a non-threatening, vulnerable form and as a stand-in for the sexually suggestive. Its modern incarnation, as a figurine, works against the familiar, antiquated imagery of the Renaissance- pairing images of nude women with the pleasure of a male spectator. Building on the varied history of men and paint, Jenn Kahn explores plasticity as point of vulnerability- not strength. By destabilizing masculine traditions, the loaded and playful symbol of the figurine provides new methods to evaluate the dialogue between form and content, observer and participant; the intimate and the infinite.

Figurines are fantastically loaded objects. Fragile, decorative, subservient, and coy; their form satisfies an artificial purpose, yet their function is often difficult to justify. These decorative objects taunt with visual duality, as Kahn's work confounds by the tension they pose. Highlighting gestures of display and the subtle culture of looking, her work investigates the super precious by revealing its critical substance.

Hang in there, Baby. 2012. Dimensions vary. Found object, pleather, wire.

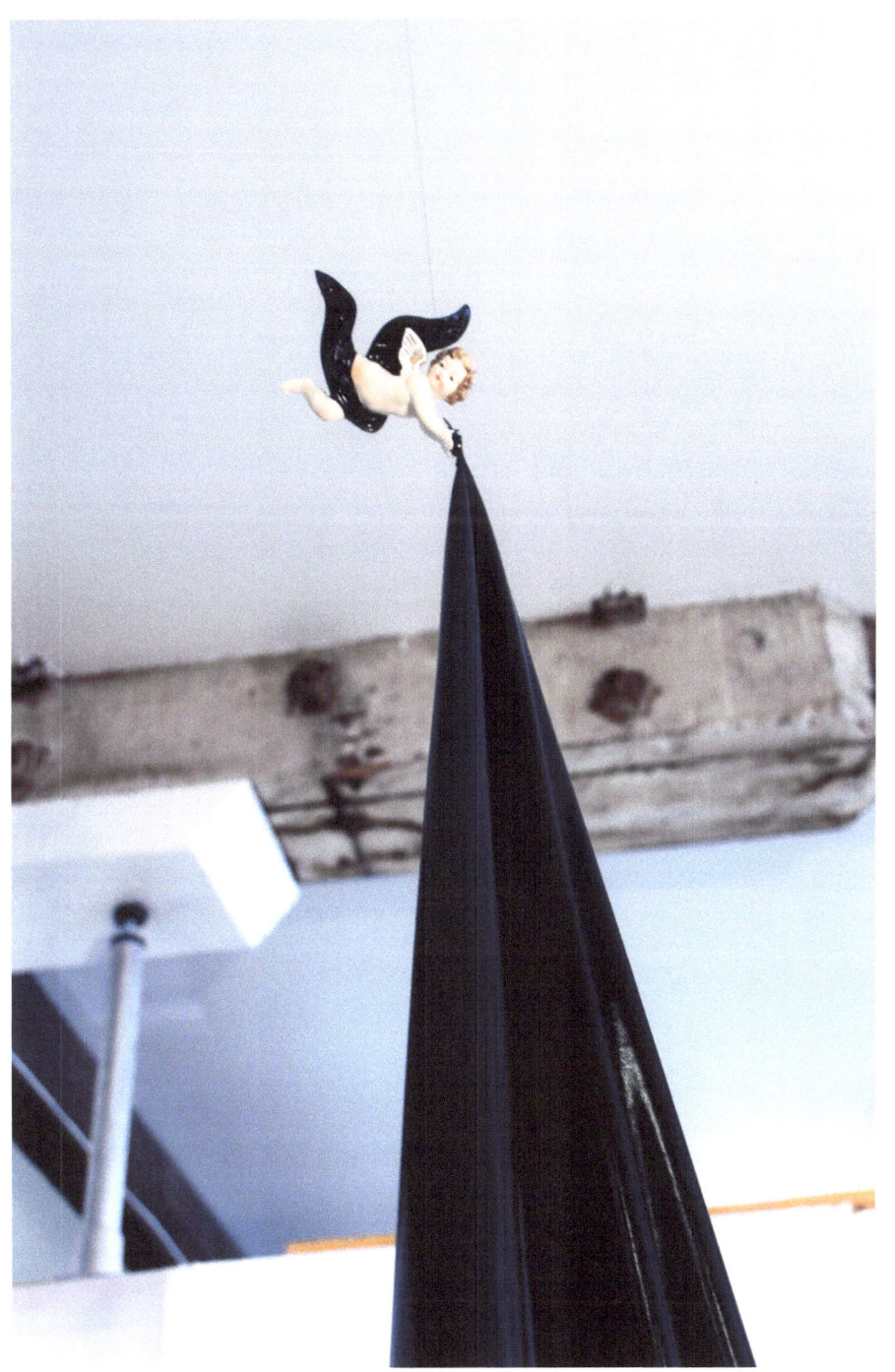

Patte Loper

During the months of the LMCC Swing Space residency Patte Loper completed a project that explores the human subconscious as a way to re-imagine architecture. Using her own sub-conscious as a model, Loper builds small struc-tures quickly as a form of automatic writing and responds to them by painting them from obser-vation. Employing backdrops drawn from her immediate environment, in this case Governors Island, the sculptures take on architectural scale and form. Loper's interest lies in finding flexible new forms by plumbing hidden weights, gravita-tional pulls and unexpected connections within subject matter.

Left: *Pieces of What,* 2012, oil on canvas, 36" x 48"
Right: *Untitled*, 2012, found objects, putty, cardboard, duct tape, 24" x 17" x 19"

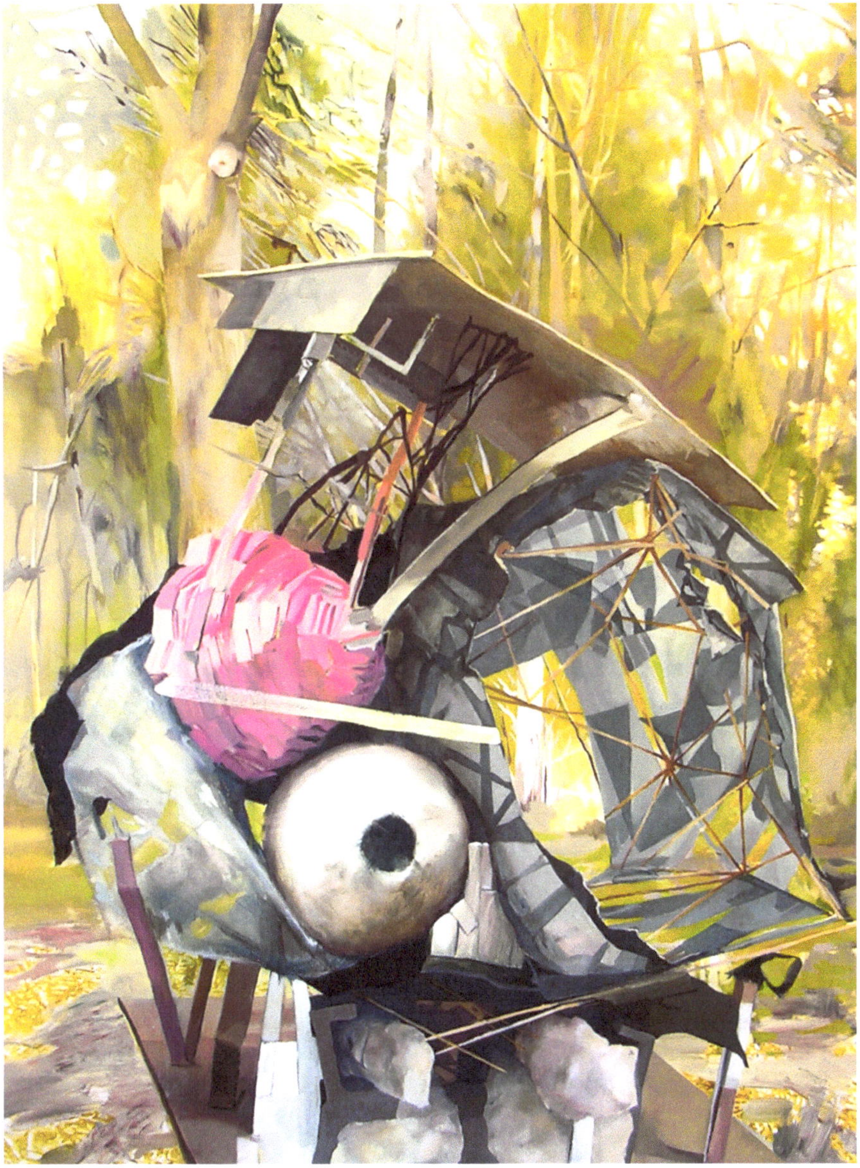

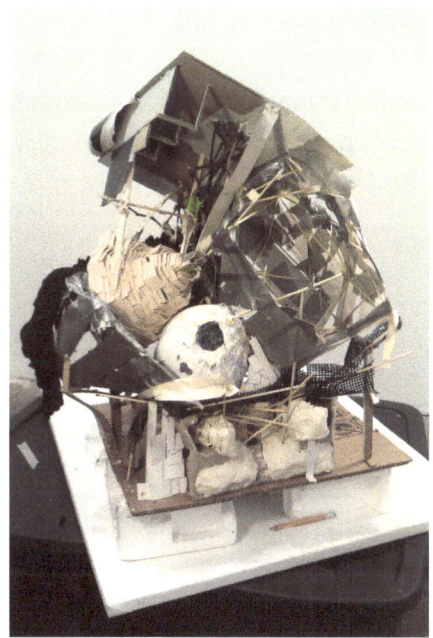

Jong Oh

In this site-specific installation, Jong Oh further expands the idea of boundaries between inner and outer spaces.

Delicately and silently responding to the site's configuration, Oh builds spatial structure by using wood, string, weight, plexiglass. Within this built structure, he allows exterior spaces to enter, through photography and the building's existing windows.

The outdoor visuals of the photographs and windows connect and intersect with objects in the installation. They exist as an element of the structure but simultaneously become a tool of visual expansion that goes beyond the installation. The outdoor elements disperse the borders of the installation and open it into a limitless space.

Reposition, Translocation, 2012, string, weight, plexiglas, wood, paint, nail, graphite, C-print, Dimensions Variable

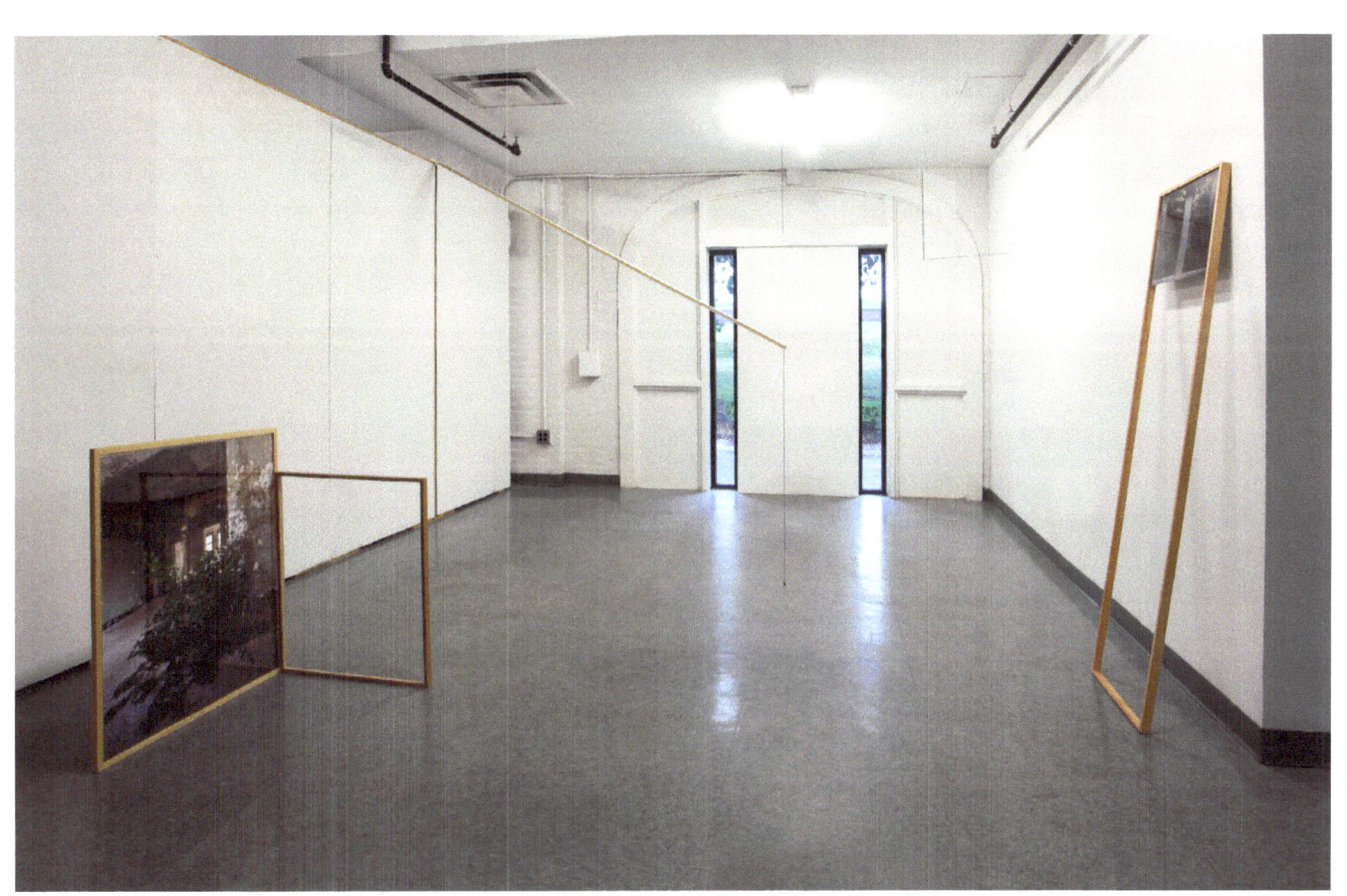

Sarada Rauch

Reinterpretation gives history more than one perspective. With this in mind, Sarada Rauch reinterprets traditional narratives using contemporary images to create modern folklore. Her aim is to excavate the buried histories within these narratives.

Rauch's work takes place in the forest, physically and metaphorically. The forest is a magical place, sheltering what is outside the ordinary, and existing on the threshold. Governors Island is like a forest in this respect, and Rauch has always wanted to use its landscape because it is such a liminal place. The strange mix of manicured park, suburban movie set houses, uninspiring residential complexes, wild overgrown areas and the pervasive military history, situates it at a sensory threshold.

Everything Rauch's work is made by hand. Combining high and low technology, and digital with the handmade, she makes static objects become animate. Her videos are a collage of lens-based footage and stop motion animation of still photographs. The soundtracks are a mix of live instruments, midi and her own voice.

Rauch's time at the Swing Space Residency on Governors Island was spent creating a video that reinterprets the final episode of the Devi Mahatmyam, utilizing the strangeness of the island. She inserted photography and video of her own sculptures into the island's landscape and recorded audio as well.

Revolution of a Gold Tornado, lenticular photograph of gold tornado spinning, 10.5 x 10.5, 2012

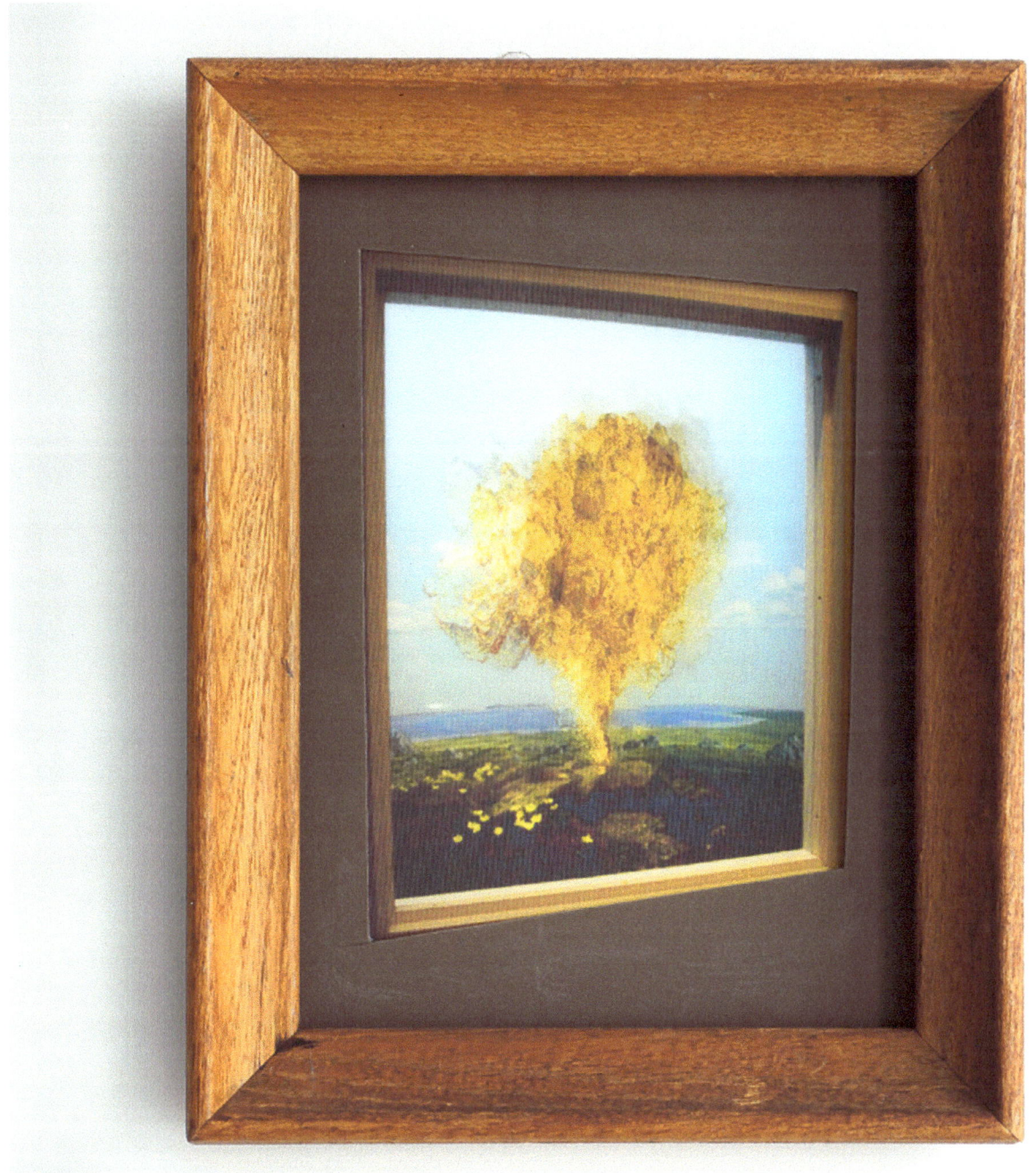

Jaye Rhee

Growing up in the 70's in Korea, Jaye Rhee was influenced by European fairy tales, particularly animation and children's books complete with happy endings. These allegories became cultural products presenting vivid depictions of a bright and fruitful world that her generation was encouraged to embrace.

This inchoate desire for «romanticized» modernity was the force that spawned a Korean industry of false images analogous to the oriental image in western art; "foreign-ness" and "western-ness" were synonyms for "modern," which meant principally the culture of Western Europe and the United States. Fragmented and adopted images such as ambiguous foreign signboards, symbols and emblems proved to be failed cultural signifiers, as they represented nothing more than the hollow, collective fantasy of my generation.

Jaye Rhee's "Heidi, a girl of Alps (Working title)" video animation takes this theme into new domains. The work directly shows the artifice of the idyllic image of what the Heidi, a girl of Apls stands for only in "our" cultural imagination.

"Heidi, a girl of Alps (working title)"
Work In Progress, Video/Animation

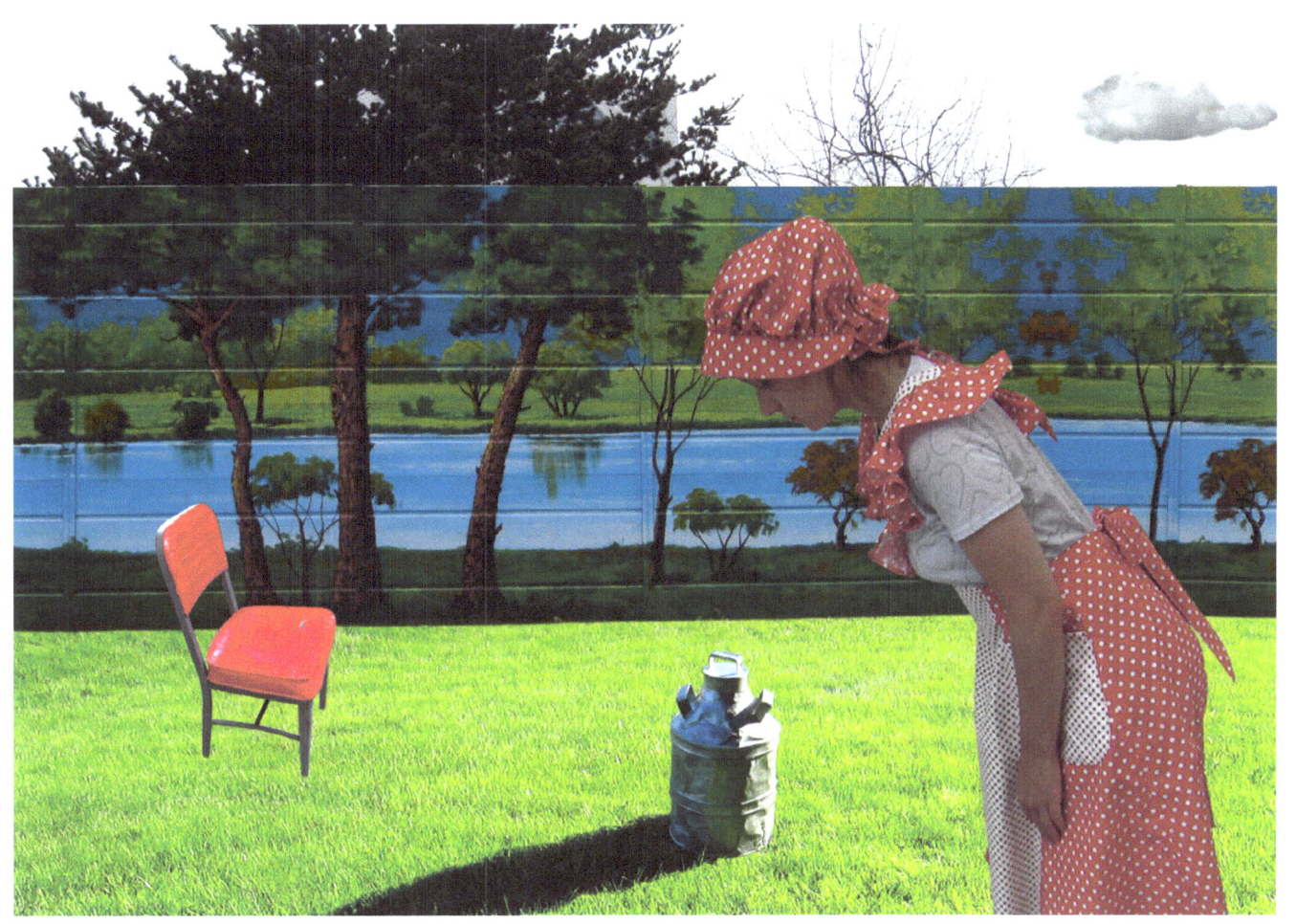

Alan Ruiz

Cultural goods come in various forms, each of which, according to Pierre Bourdieu, holds a kind of symbolic value that he labels "cultural capital." This value may appear in an *objectified* or an *institutionalized state*, but is always produced within the field of the social.

Borrowing from Bourdieu's notion of cultural capital, *Transmission* explores the symbolic and social contract surrounding the value of a work of art. In creating this work, Lower Manhattan Cultural Council Inc. agreed to loan me the four sheets of Homasote® board which normally form the partition wall of Studio 20. Stripped from their frame and of use-value, these panels were reconfigured, taking on new symbolic value as objectified cultural capital. As repurposed materials they are the vessels of collective and ghosted labor of their manufacture, former LMCC residents, and myself, illuminating a "field" of participants.

As Bourdieu writes, "cultural capital objectified in material objects [...] is *transmissible in its materiality*." These objects become containers, carrying cultural value that can be commodified. "[W]hat is transmissible" he goes on to say, "is legal ownership." Once owned, this kind of capital, one could suggest, embodies an eternal life insurance, which "confers on its holder a conventional, constant, legally guaranteed value."

But what about temporary ownership? To highlight this notion, I created an agreement between LMCC Inc., Building 110's Management, The Trust for Governors Island, and myself, to document the loan of their property not only as materials for an artwork, but as transformed objects in themselves imbued with cultural value. Therefore, the work is not static, but created through "social alchemy," that is, through a collective or triangulated relationship.

Considering that these panels have been temporarily repurposed within their usual context, both the sculpture and the contract embody the notion of an ambiguous figure: a perceptual condition describing a multi-stable image or form that reverses its figure-ground orientation. In the case of the relationship between object and institution, its physical and contractual forms embody this state of reversibility; the work is contextual, creating a relative feedback loop.

However, if collective agreements hold the power to create symbolic value, I'd like to propose that this same process could also determine its expiration. If material value is not fixed, then all that remains in these four panels as they resume their function as a partition wall is ghosted labor. Devalued and lifeless.

From *The Forms of Capital*, Pierre Bourdieu, 1986

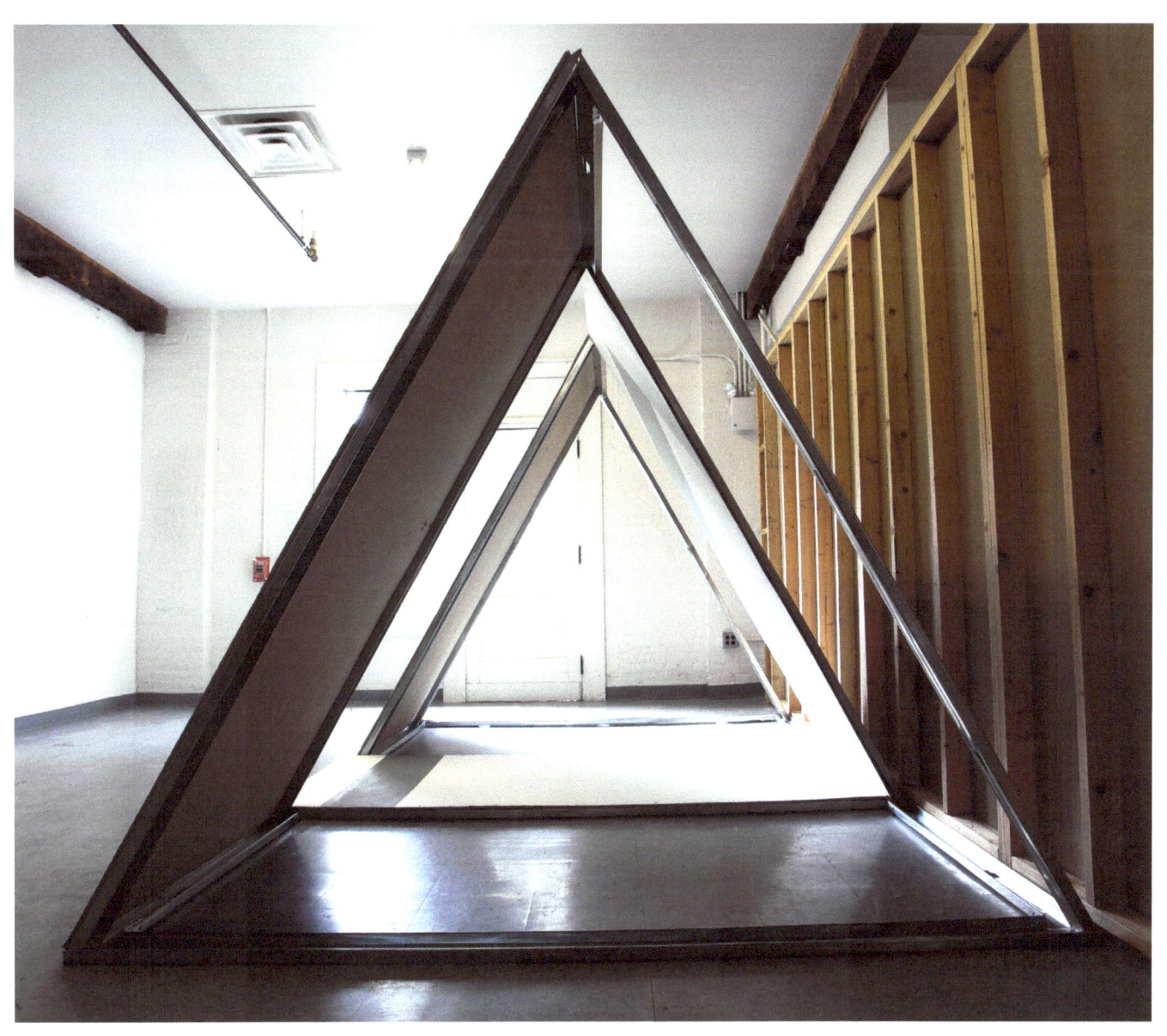

Diana Shpungin

Utilizing the mediums of drawing, sculpture and animation under an acutely conceptual framework, a minimalist aesthetic is combined with both highly personal subject matter and fanatical seriality. The work elusively investigates identity through associations to memory, mortality, loss and myth. Concerned with beauty as a sublime idea rather than as a straightforward formal element, the sentimental both seduces and repels. However, that duality has become a necessary element in Shpungin's work, always looking for balance between form/content, superstition/logic, science/sentiment and poetry/rationality.

Drawing behaves as an obsessive act employed for the exploration of memory. Many of the drawings are further used to create animation works, "purposely failed animations", or "moving stills", --never successfully animating the inanimate subject sourced from the motionless world of photography or the even more metaphorically static realm of memory. All of Shpungin's methods of working maintain a peculiar sense of longing, -- the subject matter may directly address this, a formal sensibility of tension may be employed or longing can be implied by way of self-imposed conceptual failure, --often having a purposeful yet ambiguous sense of incompletion.

For the time spent on Governors Island, Shpungin is focusing on the memory of the ocean. Recent works on this subject include "Endless Ocean", based on a photograph of the artists' father at the beach, confidently wearing a Speedo and tightly grasping onto a seagulls leg in a playful yet unconsciously sadistic manner. And also "Disappearing Act", here a blanket is seen blowing in the wind in a hypnotic like gesture. Utilizing a non-narrative structure, the work fluctuates between realism/abstraction and hovers somewhere between remembering/forgetting. The recently completed "Figure and Ground" depicts imagery that both ambiguously and cohesively represents ideas of landscape, figurative, still life and abstraction in art making. Shifting between formal, conceptual and emotional means, the elusive dark silhouette finale is to be buried in a drawing. "Recurring Tide" is an animation work in progress that considers memory in terms of the need to both forget and recall and the desire to be both welcomed and discarded.

Recurring Tide, work in progress,
hand drawn digital video animation, continuous loop
Endless Ocean, 2011,
hand drawn digital video animation, continuous loop
Figure and Ground, 2012,
hand drawn digital video animation, continuous loop
Disappearing Act, 2012,
hand drawn digital video animation, continuous loop

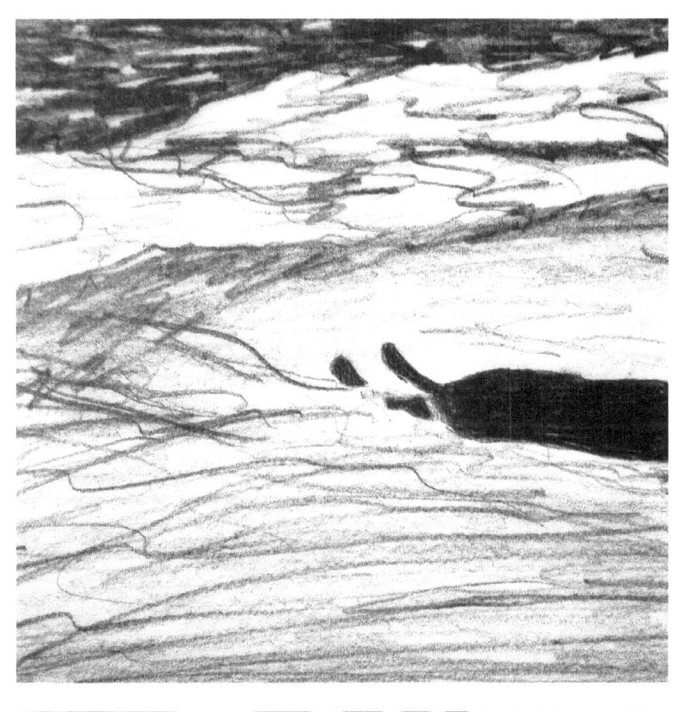
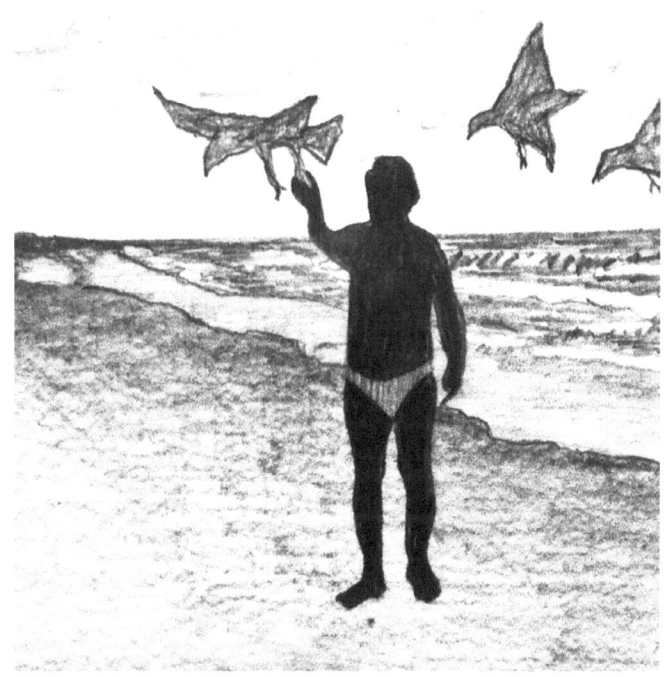

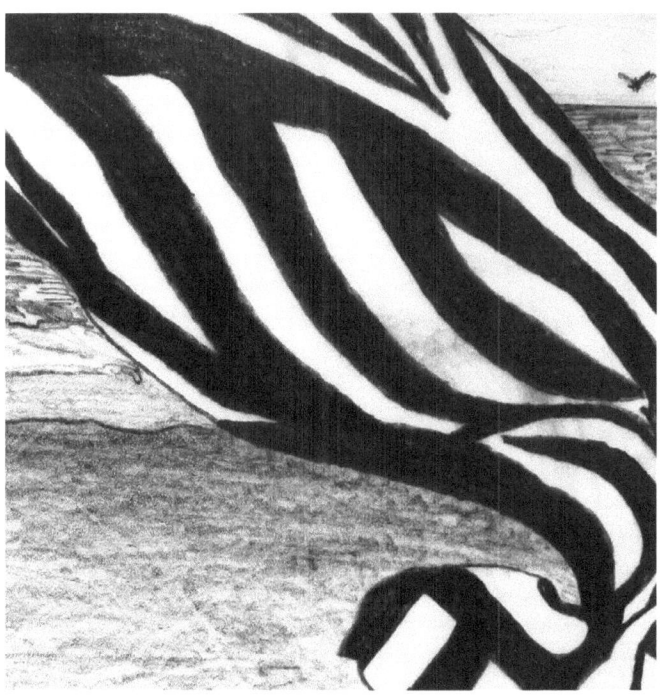
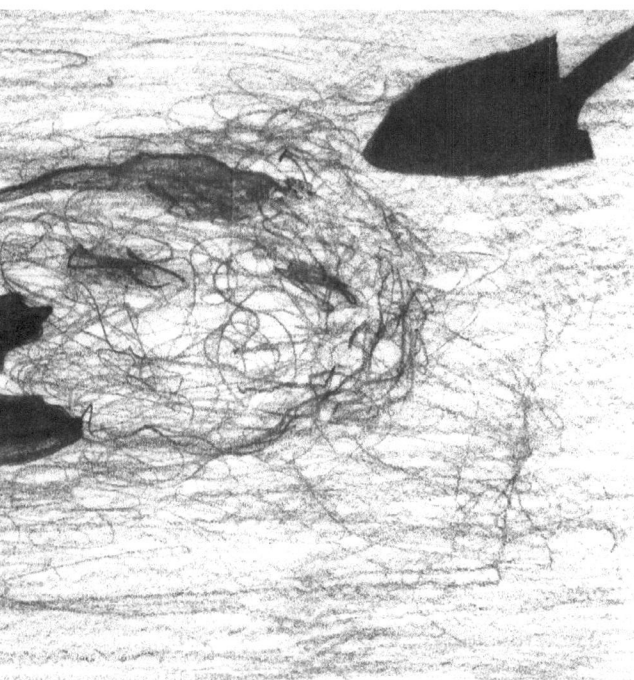

Abraham Storer

As a landscape painter, Abraham Storer understands nature as a sacred space, lending itself to silent contemplation. It depicts a foil to our mortality – a portal into something eternal and constant that extends beyond our individual lives. However, although it serves as a reflection of the divine and a place of restoration, nature also bears testament to loss - a fitting place to memorialize the dead and a stage for destructive and dumb human interventions inflicted through industry, conflict and development. This tension between the landscape as a sacred and profane space undergirds the primary concerns within his paintings.

Large objects or voids typically interrupt the space of the landscape in Storer's paintings, functioning as abstract shapes that serve as deposits of violence, loss and stillness within the context of the beautiful. However, abstraction, like nature, also serves a spiritual end, by locating the invisible within the materiality of form. This dichotomy resonates within other contrasts in his work, including interests in flatness versus volume, and nature versus urbanism.

At Governors Island, Storer located these interests in contrasts within a unique landscape: an abandoned military outpost with a seemingly pastoral character in one of America's busiest cities. In his work from the island, he focuses on a building which once served as military dormitories, finding intrigue in the abstract play of light and shadows on this banal, lonely building. The paintings become a place of escape and reveal a struggle to find spiritual relief within worldy trappings.

"Liberty," 2012, oil on canvas, 18 x 20 in.

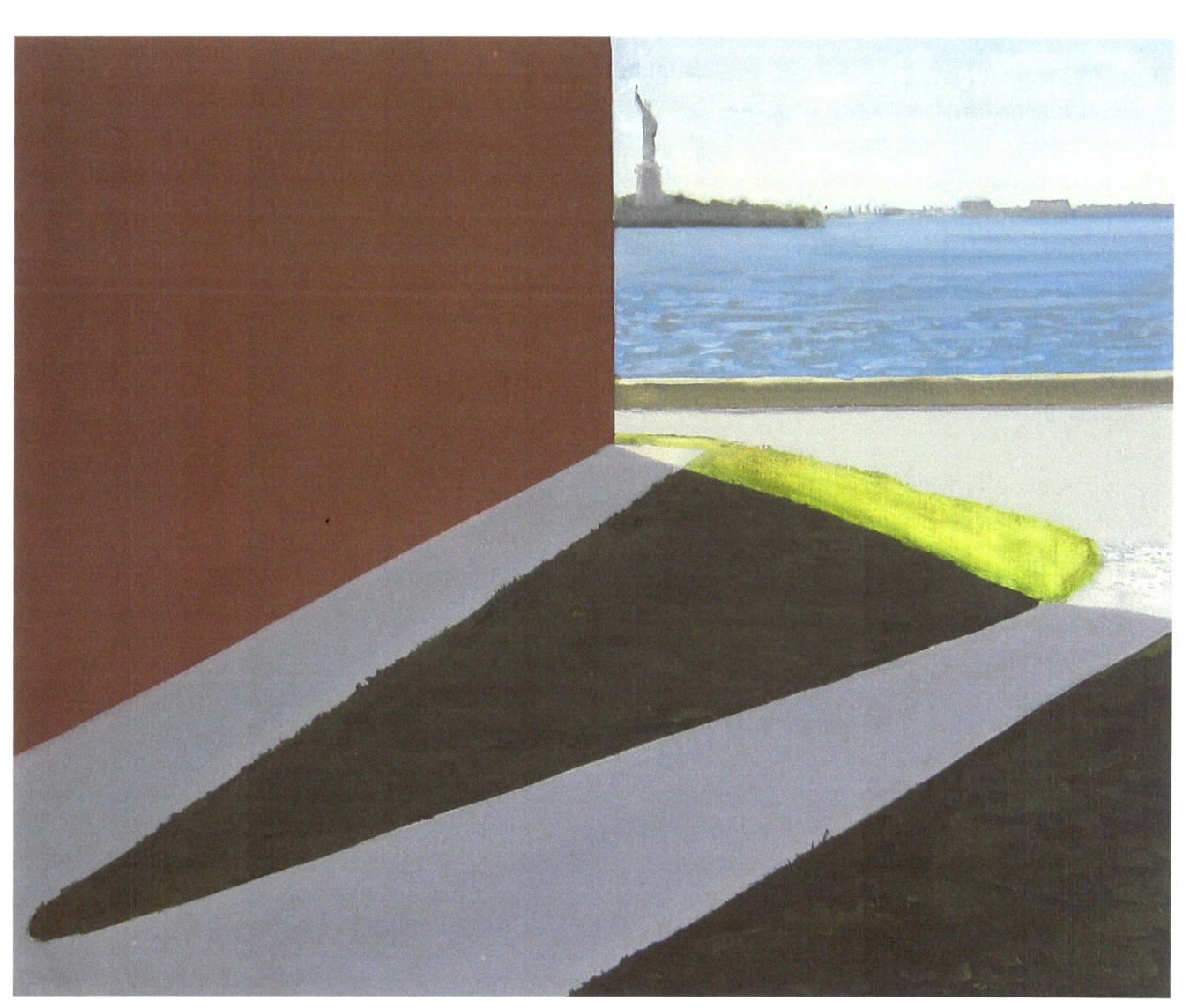

Kyoco Taniyama

Her creative inspiration is motived by the concept of ubiety - which is the quality or state of being in a space. Her interest in this concept is rooted in her history of moving because of father's job. In her childhood, she recorded the regions, address or names of her apartments in her diary to preserve her memories of where she had lived. She said, "If I didn't write them down, I would always feel lost, and this feeling of 'belonging to nowhere' is always reflected in my work." However the desire to understand one's ubiety is universal.

Kyoco Taniyama's works created on Governors Island are based on Lat/Long, a project that she started after the great earthquake and tsunami in East Japan in 2011. Lat/Long is informed by geographic latitude and longitude coordinates. Latitudinal and longitudinal numbers show us the exact point where we are on the earth, reminding us of our earthly existence. After the disaster she volunteered to help clean the affected area, and the experience inspired her to ask the question, "where are we now?" She wanted to find a way to reconfirm the ground beneath her feet and to feel the earth. In this project, she focuses on the geographical coordinates in many geographical locations. Taniyama's installations often include objects with the lat/long numbers of the exact point on trees, flowers or houses that happen to be located near the intersections of the area she is working in.

On Governors Island, Taniyama created an installation using the Manhattan view from her studio window and a work that used Castle Williams as a subject, consisting of an image, an object and sound. She also created four images of elements (water, wind, time or light and fire) that she located at simple Lat/Long points on Governors Island.

Elements N40°41'34" W74°1'6" - Fire / 2012 / c print / 30x20inch

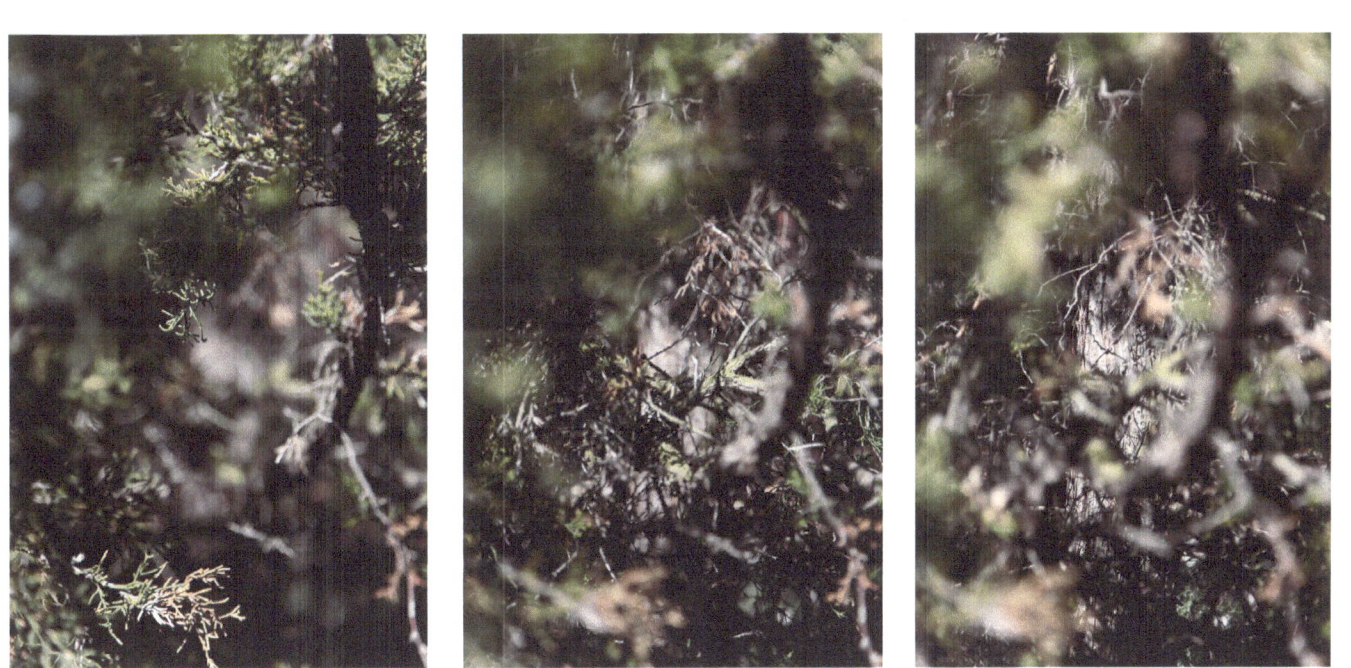

N 40°41'34"
W 74° 1' 6"

Jeanne Verdoux

Jeanne Verdoux's approach to working at this historic place was to take on the role of "artist/ archeologist" and use the island's resources, both visible and buried. At the beginning she spent most days foraging for objects that might make a physical link to the island's past. She was somewhat disappointed that the topmost layers of earth have been pretty much scraped clean since the city began developing the island as a park. However, the metal, plastic, and bakelite items she found had voices. She created a character named *Mr. Bones*, who soon inhabited her studio and the surrounding landscape as well.

His exploits called for documentation and *Mr. Bones* soon became the subject of a series of cyanotypes (...). Jeanne chose this process because the images are exposed in direct sunlight, one of the island's natural resources. As *Mr. Bones* accompanied Jeanne on her daily foraging expeditions, however, she began photographing him in color using a digital SLR camera.

The items that turned up continued to be fairly small bits left behind by previous residents. (...) Many of these formed the outline of a map of the island on the studio floor. Week by week, more characters took shape and joined the explorations and the photo shoots. By that time, the project had a name: *Made in Governors Island*. And the small size of the found items turned out to be a blessing in disguise; the characters in their studio environment, which includes the map, some furniture, and a chandelier lit by a found Christmas candle have an integral sense of scale. When photographed by Verdoux outdoors, however, they become oddly monumental.

"Jeanne Verdoux on Governors Island," by Peggy Roalf published in DART: Design Arts Daily, July 13, 2012

'Climate change', 2012, Made with objects found on Governors Island, C print, variable size

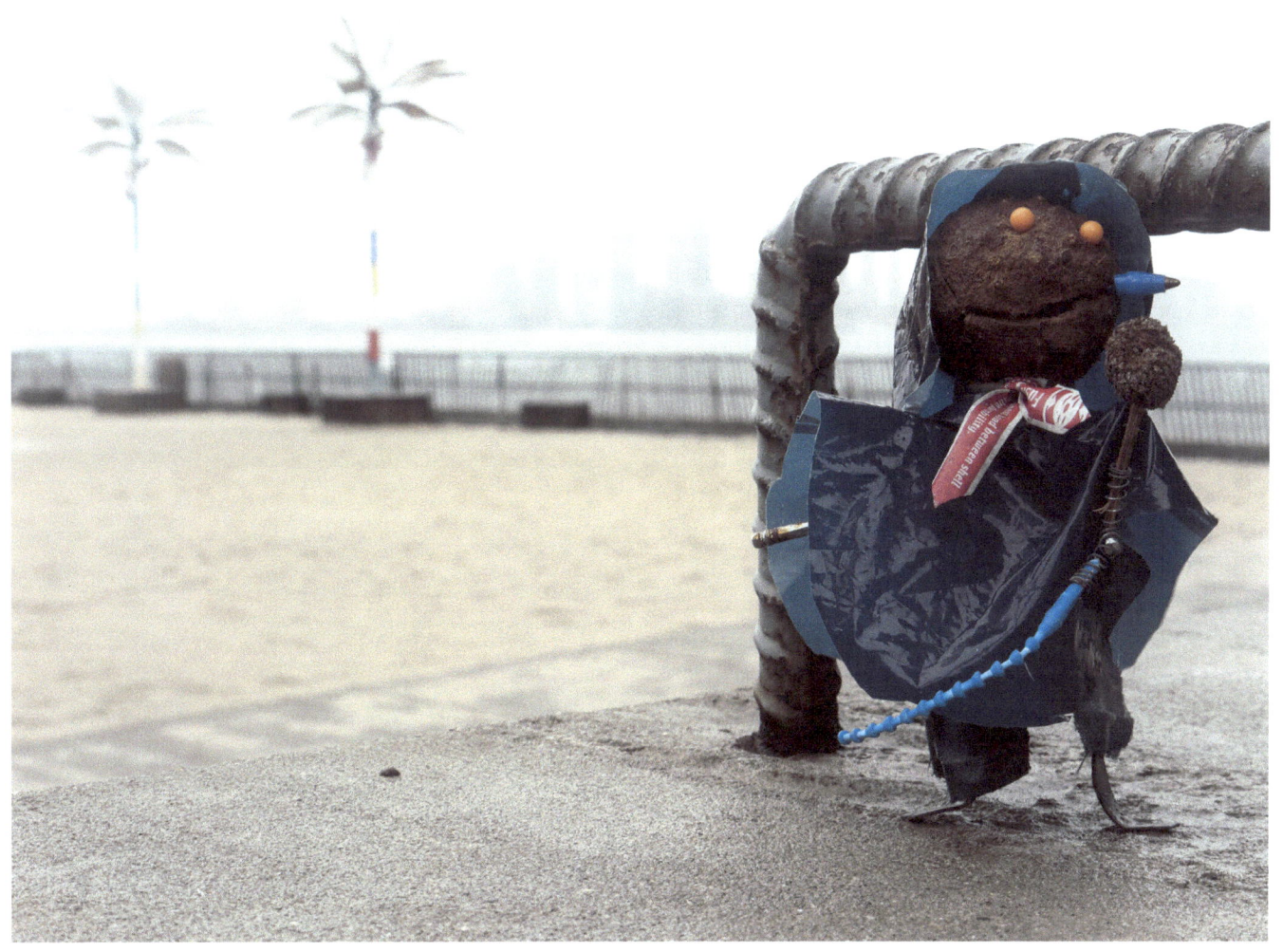

41

Jenifer Wightman

For the LMCC residency Jenifer Wightman fabricated five steel and glass frames to hold mud and water from polluted waterways in NYC. Each frame includes mud from one of the following: Hudson River (PCBs), Gowanus Canal (heavy metals), Deadhorse Bay (exposed landfill), East River (raw sewage), Newtown Creek (oil spill). Enclosed in a sculptural frame, endogenous bacteria photosynthesize pigments to create a transforming colorfield as defined by the physical and chemical conditions of the water:mud composite. The living organisms manufacturing the pigments are simultaneously the subject and substance of the 'painterly' objectification – both object and medium, both a work of art itself and a working of autopoiesis. The portrait is literal. Construction and deconstruction of molecular building blocks produce an ongoing dis/integration of form. Therefore there is not one portrait, but a series of real time/space negotiations performed by bacteria within a frame of finite natural resources. Color acts as indicator of the industry of microfauna cleaning our city.

Portraits of New York City - East River, week 10. 2012. 15"x15"x2". Mud and water from the East River, endogenous bacteria, 1 praying mantis, 5 oysters, 7 sea squirts, seaweed, 3 eggs, 4 sticks of chalk, Wall Street Journal, silicone, glass, steel.

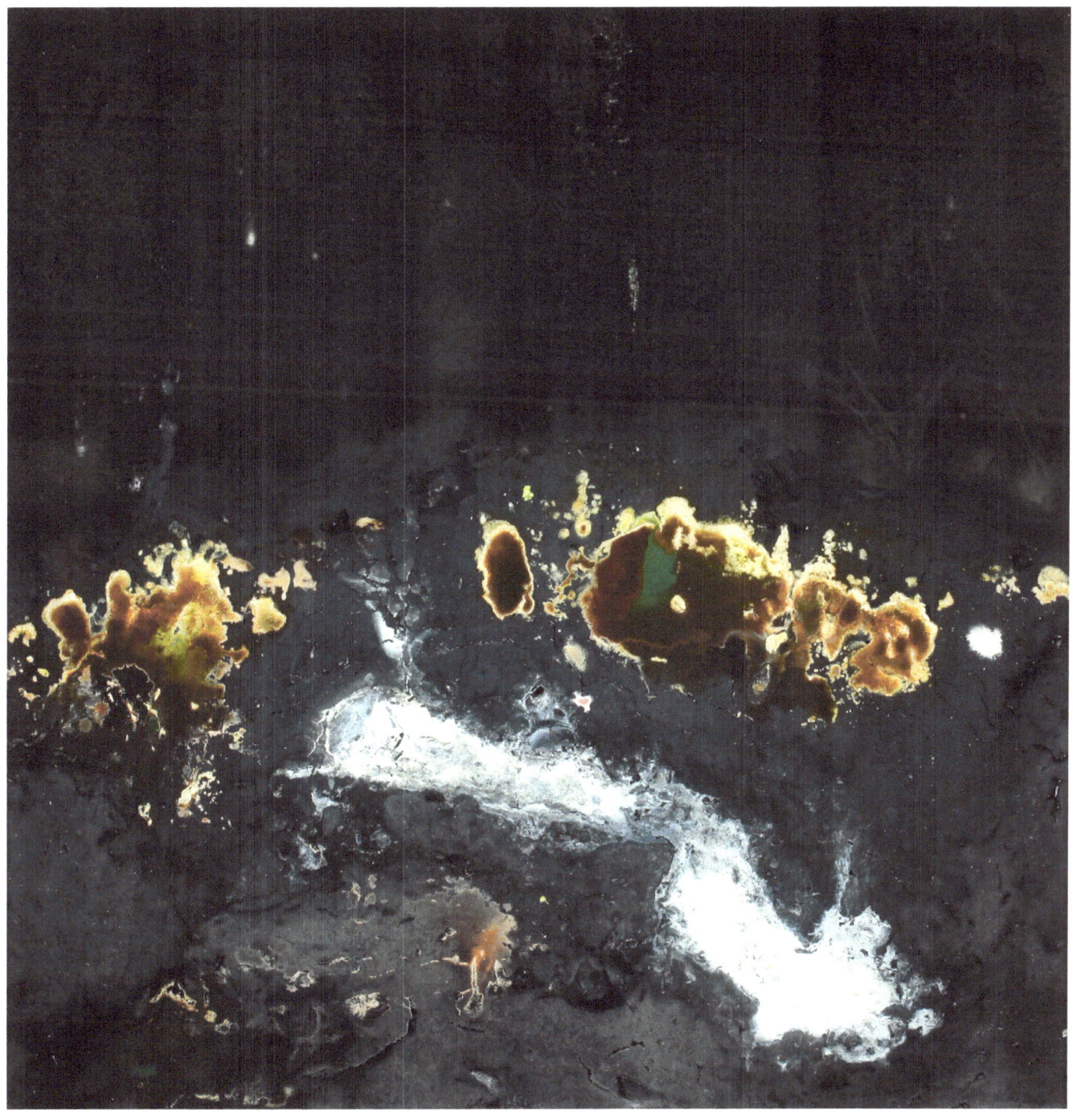

Artists' bios

Ruta Butkute

Ruta Butkute is an Amsterdam-based artist from Lithuania. Butkute has been an artist-in-residence at CBK Amsterdam Zuidoost Center of Visual Arts, BijlmAir residency (2011). She received a Start Scholarship from the Mondriaan Fund for Visual Artists (2012), and was nominated for the Gerrit Rietveld award in 2010. Butkute has received B.F.A.s from Gerrit Rietveld Academie, Vilnius Academy of Fine Arts, and Hacettepe University.
www.rutabutkute.com

Jessica Cannon

is a New York-based artist whose works explore landscapes in moments of suspension. She has exhibited at Mixed Greens, Tinlark, The Brooklyn Academy of Music, The Hudson Valley Center for Contemporary Art, and elsewhere.
www.jescannon.com

Maya Ciarrocchi

Maya Ciarrocchi's video installations present nuanced views of social, political and cultural issues, ranging from Mountaintop Removal mining in Appalachia to women's reproductive healthcare in the United States. Ciarrocchi earned a BFA in dance from SUNY Purchase and an MFA in computer art from the School of Visual Arts. She lives and works in New York City.
www.mayaciarrocchi.com

Abigail DeVille

Abigail DeVille received her MFA from Yale University in 2011 and her BFA from Fashion Institute of Technology in 2007. DeVille has exhibited a growing constellation of site-specific installations in the United States and Europe. Her most recent exhibitions include Fore at The Studio Museum, New York (2012), Future Generation Prize Exhibition at the Pinchuk Art Centre, Kiev, Ukraine (2012); First Among Equals at the ICA, Philadelphia, PA (2012); The Ungovernables at The New Museum; NY (2012); Bosh Young Talent Show at the Stedelijk Museum, 's-Hertogenbosch, Netherlands (2011). Her work has been written about in New York Magazine, The New York Times, Artforum.com, Time Out New York, CAPITAL, Philadelphia Weekly, Interview, Black Book, Nylon, Art News and Paper Magazine.
www.abigaildeville.com

Elizabeth Duffy

Elizabeth Duffy has exhibited work at the Drawing Center, the Aldrich Museum of Contemporary Art, White Columns, Elizabeth Harris Gallery, Wave Hill, The Islip Museum, and Muriel Guépin Gallery. She has been a fellow at the MacDowell Colony, Yaddo and the Bogliasco Foundation, and is the recipient of awards from the Lower Manhattan Cultural Council, NYFA, The Pollock Krasner Foundation, and the Rhode Island State Council on the Arts. Duffy lives and works in Providence, RI and Acworth, NH.
www.elizabethduffy.net

Erin Dunn

Erin Dunn's multi-disciplinary work explores the idea that, historically, female mysticism has provided spiritual and cultural power, and as the cult of fantastic female youth evolves,

her work lives in the realm of self-portrait avatars. Dunn has had solo exhibitions at Rooster Gallery NY, W139 Amsterdam and Carl Berg Gallery LA. Her work has been included in group shows at Mixed Greens Gallery NY, The Kitchen NY, The Hunter Museum of American Art TN and The New Museum, NY.
www.erinmariedunn.com

Laurie Frick

Laurie Frick draws from neuroscience to construct intricately hand-built works and installations to investigate the nature of pattern and the mind. Using her background in engineering and high-technology she explores self-tracking and human patterns. Born in Los Angeles, she lives and works in Austin, Texas and Brooklyn, New York.
www.lauriefrick.com

Marina Gutierrez

Marina Gutierrez is a multidisciplinary artist from NYC with a practice combining community based work, public and studio arts. Recent exhibits include: the Queens Museum (NYC),

Parc de la Villette (Paris), El Museo del Barrio (NYC) and an installation at Project Row Houses (Houston). She's received Joan Mitchel, NYFA and Mid-Atlantic Fellowships, a Rotunda/B.C.A.T Multi-Media Residency, and 2 NYC Arts Commission Design Awards for public projects in East Harlem and Prospect Park.
www.marinagutierrez.com

Sarah Kabot

Sarah Kabot is a Cleveland Ohio based artist whose work investigates constant states of flux and transfiguration in the built environment. Recent honors have included residencies at Headlands Center for the Arts and the Dieu Donne Workspace Program. Her work has been exhibited at Smack Mellon, Tracy Williams Ltd., Mixed Greens, the Museum of Contemporary Art Cleveland, the Drawing Center, and Tegnerforbundet in Norway.
www.sarahkabot.com

Jenn Kahn

Through serial repetition, Jenn Kahn uses sculpture and video

to highlight the visual tension between form and content; observer and participant; the intimate and the infinite. In 2011, Kahn was selected as the Van Lier Fellow and Urban Glass Visiting Artist. She has exhibited with New Art Dealers Alliance (NADA), New Museum's Festival of Ideas, Atlantic Center for the Arts, Anderson Ranch Arts Center and most recently the VLA Art + Law Residency. Kahn lives and works in Brooklyn, NY.
www.jennkahn.com

Patte Loper

Patte Loper is is a Brooklyn-based painter who experiments with sculpture and video. Loper's recent exhibitions include Still Point of the Returning World, Platform Gallery, Seattle (2011); The Sky is Burning, the Sea Aflame, Lyons Weir Gallery, New York City (2010); and Empire, The Flat- Massimo Carasi, Milan (2009), Permanent Collection, Nancy Margolis Gallery, NY (2012); Forms in Flux, Grossman Gallery, School of the Museum of Fine Arts, Boston (2012); and The Secret

Artists' bios

Language of Animals, Tacoma Art Museum, Tacoma (2011). Loper has been awarded residencies by The Virginia Center for the Creative Arts (2011) and Washington State Arts Commission Fellowship Artist Trust (2002).
www.patteloper.com

Jong Oh

Jong Oh was born in Mauritania in the West Saharan desert in 1981. Having spent most of his childhood in Spain, Oh relocated to Korea. What consistently appears in Oh's work is perception in its vagueness and delicacy, perhaps stemming from the artist's multi-cultural experience during his youth. He has exhibited at Marc Straus LLC, Art in General, BRIC Rotunda Gallery, Korean Cultural Service, Hudson Valley Center for Contemporary Art and elsewhere.
www.ohjong.com

Sarada Rauch

Sarada Rauchis a multimedia artist born in Los Angeles and based in Brooklyn, after a stint in East Germany. She received her BFA from San Francisco Art Institute and her MFA from Hunter College. Sarada has exhibited and performed at venues such as Novella Gallery in New York, RH+ Gallery in Istanbul, De La Cruz Collection, MoCA, Winkleman Gallery at Seven, in Miami, Platform Gallery in Seattle and the RISD Museum in Providence. She has also been the recipient of The Center for Book Arts Workspace Grant, the Tony Smith Fund Award and the BBK Fellowship in Saxony.
www.saradarauch.com

Jaye Rhee

work has been exhibited internationally, including Norton Museum of Art, Queens Museum of Art, Bronx Museum, Albright Knox, (U.S.), Kobe Biennale 2007, Mori Museum (Japan), Galerie Gana Beaubourg (Paris), Kyeonggi Museum of Modern Art, Cais Gallery, Pohang Steel Art Museum and Seoul Museum of Modern Art (Seoul). Awards include: Yeongang Art Award 2011 The Franklin Furnace Fund 2010 and Art Council Korea Grant 2010, Korea-America Foundation for the Arts Award 2008. In 2010, Specter Press released an artist monograph Imageless, with her work from the last 10 years and including essays by Carol Becker, Raul Zamudio, Sara Reisman and Edwin Ramoran.
www.jrhee.com

Alan Ruiz

Alan Ruiz was born in Mexico City Mexico, and lives and works in New York. Through architectural and administrative interventions, he aims to illuminate the production, transmission, or even expiration of symbolic value as a social and contextual process, similar to figure-ground perception. His work has been exhibited in both the United States and Europe. Recent group exhibitions include B-Out, Andrew Edlin Gallery, New York City (2012); The Quality of Presence, The Chelsea Hotel, New York City (2012); In Case We Don't Die KPH VOLUME, Copenhagen, (2011); and Bronx Calling Bronx Museum of Art, New York City (2011). In 2013,

he will exhibit a site-specific project at Wave Hill, NY. Ruiz received his M.F.A. from Yale University and his B.F.A. from Pratt Institute.
www.alanruiz.com

Diana Shpungin

Diana Shpunginis a NY based artist and has exhibited in international venues including: Futura Center for Contemporary Art, Prague; Tomio Koyama, Tokyo; Carrousel du Louvre, Paris; Invisible Exports, NY; Stephan Stoyanov, NY; Museum of Contemporary Art, Miami; Brooklyn Museum, NY; Sculpture Center, NY; Bass Museum, Miami; Marella Arte Contemporenea, Milan and Galerie Zurcher, Paris. Shpungin was cited in the intro of Jerry Saltz's book "Seeing out Louder" and her work has been reviewed in NY Magazine, Artforum, Art in America, The New York Times, and among others.
www.dianashpungin.blogspot.com

Abraham Storer

Abraham Storer holds an MFA in Painting from Boston University (2008) and a BA in English from Brandeis University (2003). Following his 2010 attendance at Skowhegan School of Painting and Sculpture, Storer was honored with a Fulbright Fellowship (Israel) during the 2011-2012 academic year. Storer has exhibited work in Israel, New York, Boston, and Houston.
www.abrahamstorer.com

Kyoco Taniyama

Kyoco Taniyama is a Tokyo based artist who creates works that are between art and space/community design. She is creating site-specific installations and public arts that emphasize history and character of each regions. She has been showing her works in Japan, Korea, Canada, Australia and Austria since 1999.
www.kyococo.com

Jeanne Verdoux

Jeanne Verdoux is a French artist living in Brooklyn, NY. She received an MFA from The Royal College of Art (London). Her work has been exhibited in solo and group shows at Galerie Magda Danysz (Paris), The Bronx Museum (NY), Sandra & David Bakalar Gallery (Boston), Lumen Video Festival (NY), Muriel Guepin Gallery, (NY), Frederieke Taylor Gallery (NY) and 18Gallery (Shanghai). She has received several awards including: Villa Medicis "Hors-les-Murs," The Bronx Museum AIM program and NYFA Mentoring Program for Immigrant Artists. Verdoux's work has been reviewed in The New York Times, Time-Out NY, The Boston Globe and The Village Voice.
www.jeanneverdoux.com

Jenifer Wightman

Jenifer Wightman is a biologist specializing in greenhouse gas inventories and life cycle analysis of agronomic systems. Her art practice began in 2002 and employs scientific tropes to incite curiosity of ecological phenomena. She is interested in how we might conceive of an ecological rationality by reflecting on the co-evolution of a culture and its supporting ecosystem.
www.audiblewink.com

PROJECT *Building 110* :
LMCC Artists in Residence
Fall 2012

Catalogue Design :
Jeanne Verdoux

Project Coordination and Design :
Alan Ruiz

Copyediting :
Jessica Canon, Jenn Kahn

Typefaces :
Century Schoolbook, Gotham

© 2013
ISBN: 978-1-300-60787-8

LMCC Supporters

LMCC's Public Programs are supported, in part, by Ameriprise Financial, Bloomberg Philanthropies, Charina Endowment Fund, F.B. Heron Foundation, and Lambent Foundation. LMCC's Public Programs are also supported, in part, by public funds from the New York City Department of Cultural Affairs in partnership with the City Council, and New York State Council on the Arts.

LMCC's Artist Residency Programs are supported, in part, by Andy Warhol Foundation for the Visual Arts, Bloomberg Philanthropies, Charina Endowment Fund, Cowles Charitable Trust, F.B. Heron Foundation, Jacques and Natasha Gelman Trust, Lambent Foundation, May and Samuel Rudin Family Foundation, Inc., Milton & Sally Avery Arts Foundation, New York Community Trust, and Pollock-Krasner Foundation. Swing Space is supported by the Asian Cultural Council and Mertz Gilmore Foundation.

LMCC's Artist Residency Programs are also supported, in part, by public funds from the New York City Department of Cultural Affairs in partnership with the City Council; New York State Council on the Arts; and the National Endowment for the Arts.

With special thanks to :
Melissa Levin
Will Penrose
Clare McNulty
Danielle King
Maureen McMahon
The Trust for Governors Island Staff and Management
The Governors Island Ferry Crew
Governors Island National Park Service

Lower Manhattan Cultural Council
125 Maiden Lane,
2nd Floor,
New York, NY 10038
T/ 212 219 9401
F/ 212 219 2058
www.LMCC.net

Lower Manhattan Cultural Council

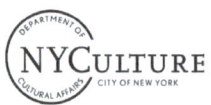

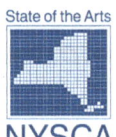

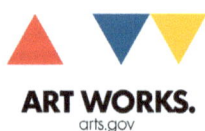

www.ingramcontent.com/pod-product-compliance
Lightning Source LLC
Chambersburg PA
CBHW051058180526
45172CB00002B/690